# Teaching Wind & Percussion Instruments

**A COURSE OF STUDY**

 MUSIC EDUCATORS NATIONAL CONFERENCE

Developed by the MENC Task Force on Band Course of Study

Donald L. Corbett, National Executive Board Liaison

Edward J. Kvet, Chair
Theodore Hadley
Edward S. Lisk
David G. Reul

# Contents

The MENC Task Force on Band Course of Study has compiled *Teaching Wind & Percussion Instruments: A Course of Study* to provide teachers with assistance in developing courses of study. In compiling this material, the Task Force members drew not only on their own training and experience but on that of music educators from across the country.

Rather than a complete or final recommended course of study, this document provides a representative approach that teachers can use in conjunction with the MENC publication *The School Music Program: Description and Standards* to improve the quality of music instruction at all levels. No endorsement of any particular method for music teaching is intended or should be inferred.

# Foreword

There is a growing concern in public school education for each discipline to identify learning outcomes appropriate for the ages of children being taught. As a result of this general educational concern, music teachers are being asked to design courses of study in the same manner as teachers in other disciplines. It is reasonable that music educators be held accountable for what is being taught in classrooms and rehearsal halls. It is also reasonable to assume that students can demonstrate what they have learned as a consequence of the instruction delivered.

Teachers often contact MENC for assistance in developing courses of study for local school districts. In the spring of 1988, a meeting was held in conjunction with MENC's National Biennial In-Service Conference in Indiana to explore the development of courses in general music, band, orchestra, and chorus. It was agreed MENC should proceed in generating such courses of study that could serve as models for any school district in the country. These courses would identify a sequence of outcomes for various ages and/or ability levels of music students.

Teachers with proven records of teaching success were selected to participate in each of the four projects. These educators spent more than two years developing materials simple and concise enough to be helpful for teachers as they plan instruction. Because each instruction area is unique, each committee was free to develop any format it felt appropriate. The four documents were never intended to be a "national" course of study; instead they offer teachers a model for the development of sequenced learning outcomes that meet their local needs.

The documents also reflect input from numerous other outstanding educators who took time to read rough drafts and respond to questionnaires. MENC hopes that teachers will find this document and the other three in the series helpful in administering sequenced music instruction that results in easily measurable learning outcomes.

Donald L. Corbett
Past President, MENC

# Acknowledgments

A project of this scope could not have been completed without the hard work of many individuals. The committee would like to express its appreciation to the following individuals who assisted with this project: Paul Alberta, Sharon Austin, Wendy Barden, Linda Becker, Michael Boday, Lisa Boortz, David Bringaman, Carolyn Bryan, Cordell Bugbee, James Coviak, Ron Cowherd, Paul Doerksen, Robb Duss, Don Farthing, Joseph Goble, James Gray, Joyce Hess, Paul Hess, Sheryl Humbert, Bill Jastrow, Charles Maupin, David Miotke, Sharon Nowak, Mel Pontious, Ben Reehl, Patricia Sahlin, Patty Schlafer, Fred Schmidt, Sharon Seymour, Laura Kautz Sindberg, Allen Slater, Kenneth Steinsultz, Theresa Tutt, and Michael Vogel.

# Preface

The members of the MENC Task Force on Band Course of Study are not so unmindful of available materials as to suggest that this book be considered a watershed document. What has been noted, however, by concerned MENC officials for years is the lack of a curricular *guide* that can be used by any school in any state as an adjunct to its own curricula documents. Many schools, it has also been noted, lack music curricular materials *entirely!* This project was initiated to fill these obvious needs and to help ameliorate curricular weaknesses.

When specific texts or works of music literature are suggested in this document, they should *not* be considered as the only available source. Also, these recommendations should not be considered as any kind of an endorsement for specific authors, composers, compositions, or texts.

The committee hopes that this document will be helpful to directors in their instruction of wind and percussion instrumentalists and will consequently result in developing increased musicality and an ever-higher quality of concert band performances.

MENC Task Force on Band Course of Study

# Overview

The work of the MENC Task Force on Band Course of Study resulted in the creation of two independent but related documents—*Teaching Wind & Percussion Instruments: A Course of Study* and the forthcoming *Activities and Materials for Wind and Percussion Study: A Sequential Approach*. Both publications are intended for use as reference guides, to be adjusted to the individual needs of the teacher or the band program. *Teaching Wind & Percussion Instruments* is recommended for those educators seeking an overview for a comprehensive wind and percussion program, while the forthcoming publication is recommended for those desiring a complete set of sample activities and materials.

Overall, both publications should be useful to all band educators, providing supplementary information and a practical guide to comprehensive wind and percussion instruction.

# Organization of the Document

*Teaching Wind & Percussion Instruments* consists of the following materials:

- *MENC Grade Cluster and Performance Level Correlations,* which provides the appropriate school grade levels for the performance levels. (See page x.)
- *Flow Chart,* which provides the philosophical foundation for the document, namely the development of musical literacy—musicianship—by means of mastering various skills and concepts integrated with the psychomotor, cognitive, and affective domains. (See page xi.)
- *Skills and Concepts—Recommended Performance Levels,* which lists the specific skills and concepts and the performance level at which each is normally introduced and reinforced.
- *Sample Activities and Materials,* which contains examples of specific activities or strategies and materials for teaching an individual skill or concept.
- *Appendix,* which contains an overview of text, method, and music references.

The *Sample Activities and Materials* listed in this book contain the following items:

Instructional Sequence: A step-by-step procedure that could be used in teaching the skill or concept.

Techniques/Devices: Specific aids one can use for teaching the skill or concept.

Checks: Those items that need to be "checked" while teaching the skill or concept.

Texts or Methods: Examples of texts or methods that may aid the teaching of the skill or concept. (See the Appendix for authors and publishers.)

Music: Examples of music or recordings that may aid the teaching of the skill or concept or that incorporate the actual skill or concept being taught. (See the Appendix for names of composers, arrangers, and publishers.)

All plans may not contain all five items. Information is included only in those areas relevant to the skill or concept.

# How to Use This Course of Study

*Teaching Wind & Percussion Instruments* is recommended for those educators seeking an overview of a comprehensive wind and percussion program. The organization, complete listing of individual skills and concepts, and recommended performance levels in this document should provide useful tools for both first-year and experienced educators.

Teachers are encouraged to use the *Skills and Concepts— Recommended Performance Levels* as a checklist throughout wind and percussion study. In interpreting these correlations, it should be noted that Level I is intended as an introductory level and is not correlated to a single school grade level. This takes into consideration the various school grade levels at which band instruction takes place. Likewise, one should not assume all school programs will achieve a Level VI performance level.

Wind and percussion educators should find this document a useful aid in organizing and planning their daily instruction activities. Experienced teachers may use the activities that best suit their individual teaching style. New teachers are encouraged to follow this model closely to ensure thorough coverage of the subject matter.

## MENC Grade Cluster / Performance Level Correlations

| School Grade Cluster | Performance Level |
| --- | --- |
| 1–3 | – |
| 4–6 | I–II |
| 6–8/7–9 | I–IV |
| 9–12 | III–VI |

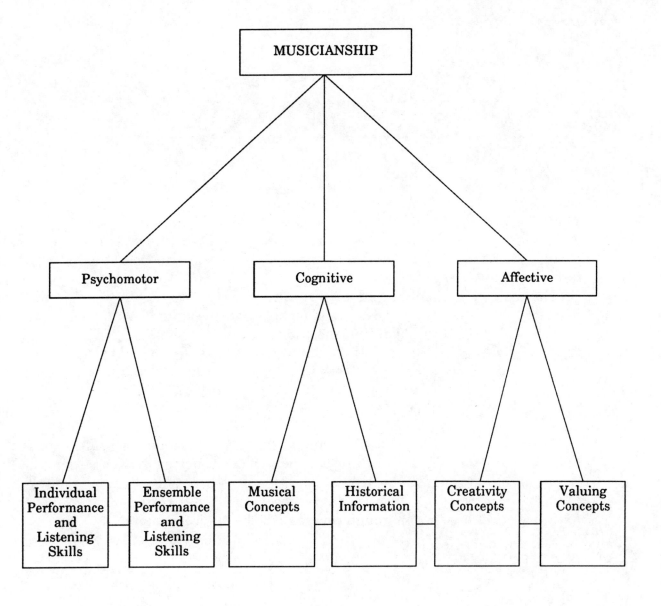

*Flow chart, showing the development of musicianship by mastering various skills and concepts integrated with the psychomotor, cognitive, and affective domains.*

# Skills and Concepts
## Recommended Performance Levels

## Individual Performance and Listening Skills

| Skill or Concept | I | II | III | IV | V | VI |
|---|---|---|---|---|---|---|
| ***Basic Wind Instrument Skills*** | I | II | III | IV | V | VI |
| Breathing (see page 21) | • | → | → | → | → | → |
| Posture | • | → | → | → | → | → |
| Tone Production/Quality | • | → | → | → | → | → |
| Balance/Blend | • | → | → | → | → | → |
| Fingerings | • | → | → | → | → | → |
| Hand Position | • | → | → | → | → | → |
| ***Advanced Wind Instrument Skills*** | I | II | III | IV | V | VI |
| Double/Triple Tonguing | | | • | • | → | → |
| Transposition (see page 23) | | | • | • | → | → |
| Flutter Tonguing | | | | | • | • |
| Quarter Tones | | | | | | • |
| Multiphonics | | | | | | • |
| ***Specific Flute/Piccolo Skills*** | I | II | III | IV | V | VI |
| Assembly (see page 25) | • | → | → | → | → | → |
| Instrument Position | • | → | → | → | → | → |
| Embouchure | • | → | → | → | → | → |
| Articulation | • | → | → | → | → | → |
| Intonation | • | → | → | → | → | → |
| Care and Maintenance | • | → | → | → | → | → |
| Vibrato | | | | • | → | → |
| Alternate Fingerings | | | • | • | → | → |

• = level at which skill or concept is normally introduced. (When more than one • appears, the skill or concept can be introduced at either level.)

→ = level at which skill or concept is normally reinforced.

*Note:* Activities and materials for skills or concepts without page numbers appear in the forthcoming *Activities and Materials for Wind and Percussion Study: A Sequential Approach.*

### Specific Oboe Skills

| | I | II | III | IV | V | V |
|---|---|---|---|---|---|---|
| Assembly | ● | → | → | → | → | → |
| Instrument Position | ● | → | → | → | → | → |
| Embouchure | ● | → | → | → | → | → |
| Articulation | ● | → | → | → | → | → |
| Intonation | ● | → | → | → | → | → |
| Care and Maintenance (see page 26) | ● | → | → | → | → | → |
| Alternate Fingerings | ● | → | → | → | → | → |
| Reed Adjustment | | ● | → | → | → | → |
| Vibrato | | | ● | ● | → | → |
| Reed Making | | | | ● | → | → |

### Specific Clarinet Skills

| | I | II | III | IV | V | VI |
|---|---|---|---|---|---|---|
| Assembly | ● | → | → | → | → | → |
| Instrument Position | ● | → | → | → | → | → |
| Embouchure | ● | → | → | → | → | → |
| Articulation | ● | → | → | → | → | → |
| Intonation | ● | → | → | → | → | → |
| Care and Maintenance | ● | → | → | → | → | → |
| Crossing the Break (see page 27) | ● | ● | → | → | → | → |
| Alternate Fingerings | | ● | ● | → | → | → |
| Reed Adjustment | | ● | ● | → | → | → |
| Throat Tones | | | ● | → | → | → |
| Transposition | | | | | ● | ● |

### Specific Bassoon Skills

| | I | II | III | IV | V | VI |
|---|---|---|---|---|---|---|
| Assembly | ● | → | → | → | → | → |
| Instrument Position | ● | → | → | → | → | → |
| Embouchure | ● | → | → | → | → | → |
| Articulation | ● | → | → | → | → | → |
| Intonation | ● | → | → | → | → | → |
| Care and Maintenance | ● | → | → | → | → | → |
| Alternate Fingerings | | ● | → | → | → | → |
| Reed Adjustment (see page 29) | | ● | ● | → | → | → |
| Vibrato | | | ● | → | → | → |
| Reed Making | | | | ● | → | → |

### Specific Saxophone Skills

| | I | II | III | IV | V | VI |
|---|---|---|---|---|---|---|
| Assembly | ● | → | → | → | → | → |
| Instrument Position (see page 30) | ● | → | → | → | → | → |
| Embouchure | ● | → | → | → | → | → |
| Articulation | ● | → | → | → | → | → |
| Intonation | ● | → | → | → | → | → |
| Care and Maintenance | ● | → | → | → | → | → |
| Alternate Fingerings | | ● | → | → | → | → |
| Reed Adjustment | | ● | → | → | → | → |
| Vibrato | | | ● | → | → | → |

| *Specific French Horn Skills* | I | II | III | IV | V | VI |
|---|---|---|---|---|---|---|
| Assembly | • | → | → | → | → | → |
| Instrument Position | • | → | → | → | → | → |
| Embouchure | • | → | → | → | → | → |
| Articulation | • | → | → | → | → | → |
| Intonation | • | → | → | → | → | → |
| Care and Maintenance | • | → | → | → | → | → |
| Right-Hand Technique | • | → | → | → | → | → |
| Lip Slurs | | • | → | → | → | → |
| Single/Double Horn | | • | • | → | → | → |
| Muting | | | • | → | → | → |
| Transposition | | | • | • | → | → |
| Glissando | | | | • | → | → |
| Stopping (see page 31) | | | | • | → | → |
| Lip Trill | | | | | • | • |

| *Specific Cornet/Trumpet Skills* | I | II | III | IV | V | VI |
|---|---|---|---|---|---|---|
| Assembly | • | → | → | → | → | → |
| Instrument Position (see page 32) | • | → | → | → | → | → |
| Embouchure | • | → | → | → | → | → |
| Articulation | • | → | → | → | → | → |
| Intonation | • | → | → | → | → | → |
| Care and Maintenance | • | → | → | → | → | → |
| Lip Slurs | | • | → | → | → | → |
| Intonation/Valve Slides | | • | • | → | → | → |
| Vibrato | | | • | → | → | → |
| Transposition | | | | • | → | → |
| Alternate Fingerings | | | | • | → | → |

| *Specific Trombone Skills* | I | II | III | IV | V | VI |
|---|---|---|---|---|---|---|
| Assembly | • | → | → | → | → | → |
| Instrument Position | • | → | → | → | → | → |
| Embouchure | • | → | → | → | → | → |
| Articulation | • | → | → | → | → | → |
| Intonation | • | → | → | → | → | → |
| Care and Maintenance | • | → | → | → | → | → |
| Lip Slurs | | • | → | → | → | → |
| Legato Tonguing (see page 33) | | • | • | → | → | → |
| Slide Technique | | • | • | → | → | → |
| Alternate Positions | | • | • | → | → | → |
| Vibrato | | | • | • | → | → |
| F-Attachment | | | • | • | → | → |
| Other Clefs | | | | • | • | → |

| *Specific Baritone/Euphonium Skills* | I | II | III | IV | V | VI |
|---|---|---|---|---|---|---|
| Assembly | • | → | → | → | → | → |
| Instrument Position | • | → | → | → | → | → |
| Embouchure | • | → | → | → | → | → |
| Articulation | • | → | → | → | → | → |
| Intonation | • | → | → | → | → | → |
| Care and Maintenance | • | → | → | → | → | → |
| Lip Slurs | | • | → | → | → | → |
| Vibrato (see page 34) | | | • | → | → | → |
| Fourth-Valve Technique | | | • | • | → | → |

| *Specific Tuba/Sousaphone Skills* | I | II | III | IV | V | VI |
|---|---|---|---|---|---|---|
| Assembly | • | → | → | → | → | → |
| Instrument Position | • | → | → | → | → | → |
| Embouchure | • | → | → | → | → | → |
| Articulation | • | → | → | → | → | → |
| Intonation | • | → | → | → | → | → |
| Care and Maintenance | • | → | → | → | → | → |
| Lip Slurs | | • | → | → | → | → |
| Vibrato | | | • | → | → | → |
| Fourth-Valve Technique (see page 35) | | | • | • | → | → |

| *Specific Snare Drum Skills* | I | II | III | IV | V | VI |
|---|---|---|---|---|---|---|
| Assembly | • | → | → | → | → | → |
| Instrument / Playing Position | • | → | → | → | → | → |
| Grip (Matched or Traditional) | • | → | → | → | → | → |
| Articulation/Sticking | • | → | → | → | → | → |
| Care and Maintenance | • | → | → | → | → | → |
| Single Stroke | • | → | → | → | → | → |
| Double Stroke | • | → | → | → | → | → |
| Paradiddle (see page 36) | • | → | → | → | → | → |
| Multiple Stroke Rolls (Buzz Roll) | • | → | → | → | → | → |
| Alt. and Nonalt. Double Stroke Rolls (5, 7, 9), Open and Closed | • | • | → | → | → | → |
| Tone Production | • | • | → | → | → | → |
| Tuning | | • | → | → | → | → |
| Flams | | • | → | → | → | → |
| Rim Shot and Tap | | • | → | → | → | → |
| Ruff | | | • | → | → | → |
| Flam-A-Cue | | | • | → | → | → |
| Flam-Paradiddle | | | • | • | → | → |
| Double Paradiddle | | | • | • | → | → |
| Single, Double, Triple Ratamacue | | | • | • | → | → |
| Flam Accent #1, #2 | | | • | • | → | → |
| Single Drag | | | | • | • | → |
| Drag Paradiddle #2 | | | | • | • | → |
| Flam-Tap | | | | • | • | → |
| Advanced Rudiments | | | | • | • | • |

| Specific Keyboard Percussion Skills | I | II | III | IV | V | VI |
|---|---|---|---|---|---|---|
| Assembly | • | → | → | → | → | → |
| Body Position | • | → | → | → | → | → |
| Grip | • | → | → | → | → | → |
| Hand Position | • | → | → | → | → | → |
| Articulation/Sticking | • | → | → | → | → | → |
| Care and Maintenance | • | → | → | → | → | → |
| Tone Production | • | • | → | → | → | → |
| Two-Mallet Technique | | • | → | → | → | → |
| Mallet Selection | | • | • | → | → | → |
| Rolls | | • | • | → | → | → |
| Sustain Pedal Technique | | | | • | → | → |
| Three- / Four-Mallet Technique | | | | | • | • |

| Specific Timpani Skills | I | II | III | IV | V | VI |
|---|---|---|---|---|---|---|
| Instrument / Playing Position | • | → | → | → | → | → |
| Grip | • | → | → | → | → | → |
| Articulation/Sticking | • | → | → | → | → | → |
| Care and Maintenance | • | → | → | → | → | → |
| Tone Production | | • | → | → | → | → |
| Tuning/Ear Training | | • | • | → | → | → |
| Mallet Selection | | • | • | → | → | → |
| Rolls | | • | • | → | → | → |
| Damping/Muffling | | | • | • | → | → |
| Special Effects (Glissando, *sfp* Rolls) | | | • | • | • | → |

| Specific Bass Drum Skills | I | II | III | IV | V | VI |
|---|---|---|---|---|---|---|
| Assembly | • | → | → | → | → | → |
| Instrument / Playing Position | • | → | → | → | → | → |
| Care and Maintenance | • | → | → | → | → | → |
| Damping | • | → | → | → | → | → |
| Mallet Technique | • | → | → | → | → | → |
| Tone Production | | • | → | → | → | → |
| Tuning | | • | → | → | → | → |
| Mallet Selection | | • | • | → | → | → |
| Rolls | | | • | → | → | → |

| Specific Auxiliary Percussion Skills | I | II | III | IV | V | VI |
|---|---|---|---|---|---|---|
| Instrument / Playing Position | • | → | → | → | → | → |
| Care and Maintenance | • | → | → | → | → | → |
| Crash Cymbal Technique | • | → | → | → | → | → |
| Triangle Technique | • | → | → | → | → | → |
| Tambourine Technique | • | → | → | → | → | → |
| Suspended Cymbal Technique | | • | → | → | → | → |
| Tom-Tom Technique | | • | → | → | → | → |
| Mallet Selection | | • | • | → | → | → |
| Gong (Tam-Tam) Technique | | • | • | → | → | → |
| Latin Percussion Technique | | | • | • | → | → |

| | I | II | III | IV | V | VI |
|---|---|---|---|---|---|---|
| Hand Drum Technique | | | | • | • | → → |
| Special Effects Percussion (e.g., slap stick) | | | | • | • | → |

| **Specific Drum Set Skills** | I | II | III | IV | V | VI |
|---|---|---|---|---|---|---|
| Assembly | | • | • | → | → | → |
| Instrument / Playing Position | | • | • | → | → | → |
| Care and Maintenance | | • | • | → | → | → |
| Pedal Technique (Coordinated Independence) | | • | • | → | → | → |
| Hi-Hat | | • | • | → | → | → |
| Brushes | | • | • | → | → | → |
| Cymbals | | • | • | → | → | → |

## Ensemble Performance and Listening Skills

| **Skill** | I | II | III | IV | V | VI |
|---|---|---|---|---|---|---|
| Breathing | • | → | → | → | → | → |
| Posture | • | → | → | → | → | → |
| Listening (see page 39) | • | → | → | → | → | → |
| Entrance/Release | • | → | → | → | → | → |
| Balance/Blend | • | • | → | → | → | → |
| Intonation | • | • | → | → | → | → |
| Tone Quality/Focus | • | • | → | → | → | → |
| Rhythm/Pulse | • | • | → | → | → | → |

## Musical Concepts—Rhythm

| **Pulse/Beat** | I | II | III | IV | V | VI |
|---|---|---|---|---|---|---|
| Steady Beat | • | → | → | → | → | → |
| Measurement of Silence | • | → | → | → | → | → |
| Flexible (e.g., Rubato, Tenuto) | | • | • | → | → | → |
| Free (e.g., Improvisation, Cadenza) | | | • | • | → | → |

| **Time Signature/Rhythmic Notations** | I | II | III | IV | V | VI |
|---|---|---|---|---|---|---|
| 4/4 2/4 3/4   o — ♩ — ♩ ⸾ | • | → | → | → | → | → |
| 4/4 2/4 3/4   Ties ♩♩ | • | → | → | → | → | → |
| 4/4 2/4 3/4   ♫ ⸲ | • | → | → | → | → | → |
| 4/4 2/4 3/4   ♩. ♪ | • | → | → | → | → | → |
| 2/2 ¢   o — ♩ — ♩ ⸾ | • | • | → | → | → | → |
| 3/8 (in 3) 6/8 (in 6)   ♩. ♩. ♫♫ ♪♪ | • | • | → | → | → | → |
| 4/4 2/4 3/4   ♬ ♬ ♫ ⸲ | • | • | → | → | → | → |
| 4/4 2/4 3/4   ♫ | • | | → | → | → | → |
| 2/8 3/8 4/8 (fast 6/8, 9/8, 12/8)   ♩. ♩. ♬ ♪♪ o. ♫♫ (see page 43) | • | → | → | → | → | → |

| | | I | II | III | IV | V | VI |
|---|---|---|---|---|---|---|---|
| 4/4 2/4 3/4 | ♪ ♩ ♪ | | • | • | → | → | → |
| 4/4 2/4 3/4 | (triplet eighths) | | • | • | → | → | → |
| 4/4 2/4 3/4 | (triplet quarters) | | • | • | • | • | → |
| Any Time Signature | Smaller Subdivisions (e.g., ♫ ) | | | | • | • | • |
| Any Time Signature | Effect Notation (e.g., ♩, ♩) | | | | • | • | → |
| | Free Time Concepts | | | | • | • | • |
| Any Time Signature | Rhythmic Abbreviations (e.g., ♪) | | | | | • | • |
| Any Time Signature | Mixed Groupings (e.g., ♫♫♫ ) | | | | | • | • |

## Meter

| | I | II | III | IV | V | VI |
|---|---|---|---|---|---|---|
| 4/4 | • | → | → | → | → | → |
| 3/4 | • | → | → | → | → | → |
| 2/4 | • | → | → | → | → | → |
| 2/2 | • | • | → | → | → | → |
| 6/8 in 6 | • | • | → | → | → | → |
| 3/8 in 3 (see page 46) | • | • | → | → | → | → |
| 6/8 in 2 | • | • | → | → | → | → |
| 3/8 in 1 | • | • | → | → | → | → |
| Changing Meters | • | • | → | → | → | → |
| 9/8 in 3 | | • | • | → | → | → |
| 12/8 in 4 | | • | • | → | → | → |
| 5/4 in 2 ( ♩. ♩ or ♩ ♩. ) | | • | • | → | → | → |
| 3/4 in 1 | | | • | • | → | → |
| Compound, Asymmetric, Symmetric | | | • | • | → | → |
| Hemiola (3:2) | | | | | • | • |

## Tempo

| | I | II | III | IV | V | VI |
|---|---|---|---|---|---|---|
| Allegro | • | → | → | → | → | → |
| Moderato | • | → | → | → | → | → |
| Andante | • | → | → | → | → | → |
| Metronome Markings (e.g., ♩ =120) | • | • | → | → | → | → |
| Allegretto | | • | • | → | → | → |
| Andantino | | • | • | → | → | → |
| Lento | | • | • | → | → | → |
| Presto | | | • | • | → | → |
| Vivace | | | • | • | → | → |
| Adagio | | | • | • | → | → |
| Largo | | | • | • | → | → |
| Larghetto | | | | • | • | → |
| Grave | | | | • | • | → |
| Vivo | | | | | • | → |

# Musical Concepts—Melody

| *Melodic Notation/Terminology* | | I | II | III | IV | V | VI |
|---|---|---|---|---|---|---|---|
| Fine | | • | → | → | → | → | → |
| Phrase | | • | → | → | → | → | → |
| A tempo, Tempo I, Tempo Primo | | • | → | → | → | → | → |
| First and Second Endings | | • | → | → | → | → | → |
| Measure Repeat | ⁒ | • | → | → | → | → | → |
| Repeat Signs | ‖: :‖ | • | → | → | → | → | → |
| Treble Clef | 𝄞 | • | → | → | → | → | → |
| Coda Sign | ⊕ | • | → | → | → | → | → |
| Caesura | // | • | → | → | → | → | → |
| Fermata | 𝄐 | • | → | → | → | → | → |
| Breath Mark | ' | • | → | → | → | → | → |
| Tie | ⌢ | • | → | → | → | → | → |
| Slur | ⌣ | • | → | → | → | → | → |
| Sharp | ♯ | • | → | → | → | → | → |
| Natural | ♮ | • | → | → | → | → | → |
| Flat | ♭ | • | → | → | → | → | → |
| Bass Clef | 𝄢 | • | → | → | → | → | → |
| Extended Rests | ⊢— 12 —⊣ | • | → | → | → | → | → |
| Accidentals | | • | → | → | → | → | → |
| Da Capo (D.C.) | | • | • | → | → | → | → |
| Dal Segno (D.S.) | | • | • | → | → | → | → |
| D.C. al Fine | | • | • | → | → | → | → |
| Soli | | • | • | → | → | → | → |
| Tutti | | • | • | → | → | → | → |
| Alla Breve | ¢ | | • | → | → | → | → |
| Middle C | | | • | → | → | → | → |
| Chromatic | | | • | → | → | → | → |
| Coda | | | • | → | → | → | → |
| Enharmonic | | | • | → | → | → | → |
| Simile | | | • | → | → | → | → |
| G.P. (Grand Pause) | | | • | → | → | → | → |
| Arpeggio | | | • | • | → | → | → |
| L'istesso Tempo | | | • | • | → | → | → |
| Meno | | | • | • | → | → | → |
| Molto | | | • | • | → | → | → |
| Più | | | • | • | → | → | → |
| Sforzando (*sfz*) | | | • | • | → | → | → |
| C Clef | 𝄡 | | | • | → | → | → |

| | | I | II | III | IV | V | VI |
|---|---|---|---|---|---|---|---|
| Double Flat | ♭♭ | | | • | → | → | → |
| *tr* | | | | • | → | → | → |
| *8va* | | | | • | → | → | → |
| Double Sharp | | | | • | → | → | → |
| Divisi | | | | • | → | → | → |
| Grace Note | | | | • | → | → | → |
| Loco | | | | • | → | → | → |
| Ossia | | | | • | → | → | → |
| Ottava | | | | • | → | → | → |
| Tacet | | | | • | → | → | → |
| Glissando (see page 47) | | | | • | • | → | → |
| Sempre | | | | • | • | → | → |
| Volti Subito (v.s.) | | | | • | • | → | → |
| Subito | | | | • | • | → | → |
| Morendo | | | | • | • | → | → |
| Segue | | | | | • | → | → |
| Ma Non Troppo | | | | | • | → | → |
| Sans | | | | | • | → | → |
| Quasi | | | | | • | → | → |
| Attaca | | | | | • | • | → |
| A Piacere | | | | | • | • | → |
| Senza | | | | | • | • | → |
| Mordent | | | | | • | • | → |
| Turn | | | | | • | • | → |
| Nontraditional Notation Systems | | | | | | • | • |

| *Interval* | I | II | III | IV | V | VI |
|---|---|---|---|---|---|---|
| M2, m2 (Whole-, Half-Step) | • | • | → | → | → | → |
| M3, m3 | • | • | → | → | → | → |
| P4, P5 | • | • | → | → | → | → |
| Octave | • | • | → | → | → | → |
| M6, m6 | | • | • | → | → | → |
| M7, m7 | | • | • | → | → | → |
| Compound Intervals | | | • | • | → | → |

| *Key Signatures (Concert Pitch)* | I | II | III | IV | V | VI |
|---|---|---|---|---|---|---|
| B♭ | • | → | → | → | → | → |
| E♭ | • | → | → | → | → | → |
| F | • | → | → | → | → | → |
| g minor | • | • | → | → | → | → |
| c minor (see page 48) | • | • | → | → | → | → |
| A♭ | | • | → | → | → | → |
| C/a minor | | • | → | → | → | → |
| d minor | | • | → | → | → | → |
| f minor | | | • | → | → | → |
| G♭/e♭ minor | | | • | → | → | → |
| D♭/b♭ minor | | | • | → | → | → |
| G/e minor | | | • | → | → | → |

| | I | II | III | IV | V | VI |
|---|---|---|---|---|---|---|
| D / b minor | | | • | • | → | → |
| A / f♯ minor | | | | • | • | → |
| E / c♯ minor | | | | • | • | → |
| B / g♯ minor | | | | | • | • |
| F♯/d♯ minor | | | | | • | • |
| C♯/a♯ minor | | | | | • | • |
| C♭/a♭ minor | | | | | • | • |

| *Scales (Concert Pitch)* | I | II | III | IV | V | VI |
|---|---|---|---|---|---|---|
| B♭ major | • | → | → | → | → | → |
| E♭ major | • | → | → | → | → | → |
| C major | • | → | → | → | → | → |
| A♭ major | • | → | → | → | → | → |
| B♭ chromatic | • | • | → | → | → | → |
| C natural, melodic, and harmonic minor | • | • | → | → | → | → |
| F major | | • | → | → | → | → |
| g (all forms) | | • | → | → | → | → |
| E♭ chromatic | | • | → | → | → | → |
| f (all forms) | | • | • | → | → | → |
| a (all forms) | | • | • | → | → | → |
| D♭ chromatic | | • | • | → | → | → |
| d (all forms) | | • | • | → | → | → |
| D♭ / b♭ (all forms) | | • | • | → | → | → |
| G♭ / e♭ (all forms) | | | • | • | → | → |
| C♭ / a♭ (all forms) | | | • | • | → | → |
| G / e (all forms) | | | • | • | → | → |
| D / b (all forms) | | | • | • | → | → |
| A / f♯ (all forms) | | | • | • | → | → |
| E / c♯ (all forms) | | | • | • | → | → |
| B / g♯ (all forms) | | | • | • | → | → |
| F♯ / d♯ (all forms) | | | • | • | → | → |
| C♯ / a♯ (all forms) | | | • | • | → | → |

| *Phrase* | I | II | III | IV | V | VI |
|---|---|---|---|---|---|---|
| Two Bar | • | → | → | → | → | → |
| Four Bar | • | → | → | → | → | → |
| Anacrusis (Pick-Up) | • | • | → | → | → | → |
| Antecedent / Consequent (e.g., Question and Answer) | • | • | → | → | → | → |
| Repetition/Contrast | • | • | → | → | → | → |
| Asymmetrical | | • | • | → | → | → |

# Musical Concepts—Harmony

| *Scale Systems* | I | II | III | IV | V | VI |
|---|---|---|---|---|---|---|
| Scale | • | → | → | → | → | → |
| Key/Key Signature | • | → | → | → | → | → |
| Major/Minor | • | • | → | → | → | → |
| Diatonic/Chromatic | • | • | → | → | → | → |
| Pentatonic | | | • | • | → | → |

| | I | II | III | IV | V | VI |
|---|---|---|---|---|---|---|
| Blues Scale | | | • | • | → | → |
| Whole-Tone Scale | | | | • | → | → |
| Ethnic Scale Systems (e.g., Eastern, Slavic) | | | | | • | • |
| Synthetic Scales | | | | | • | • |

| Tonal Systems | I | II | III | IV | V | VI |
|---|---|---|---|---|---|---|
| Major/Minor | • | • | → | → | → | → |
| Dorian/Mixolydian/Other Modes (see page 49) | | | • | • | → | → |
| Polytonality/Bitonality | | | | • | • | → |
| Serialism/Atonality | | | | • | • | → |

| Chords | I | II | III | IV | V | VI |
|---|---|---|---|---|---|---|
| Major/Minor | • | • | → | → | → | → |
| Diminished/Augmented | | • | • | → | → | → |
| Major Seventh | | | • | → | → | → |
| Other Seventh Chords | | | | • | • | → |
| Polychords | | | | • | • | → |
| Quintal/Quartal | | | | • | • | • |
| Expanded Chords (e.g., 9th, 11th, 13th) | | | | • | • | • |
| Clusters/Other Non-Tertian Chords | | | | | • | • |

| Other Harmonic Concepts | I | II | III | IV | V | VI |
|---|---|---|---|---|---|---|
| Dissonance/Consonance | • | • | → | → | → | → |
| Overtone Series | | • | • | → | → | → |
| Modulation | | | • | • | → | → |
| Progression (see page 50) | | | | • | • | → |
| Harmonic Rhythm | | | | • | • | → |

# Musical Concepts—Form

| Compositional Devices | I | II | III | IV | V | VI |
|---|---|---|---|---|---|---|
| Repetition/Contrast | • | → | → | → | → | → |
| Cadence | • | → | → | → | → | → |
| Section | • | → | → | → | → | → |
| Homophony (see page 51) | • | → | → | → | → | → |
| Coda | • | • | → | → | → | → |
| Introduction | • | • | → | → | → | → |
| Polyphony/Counterpoint | • | • | → | → | → | → |
| Heterophony | • | • | → | → | → | → |
| Ostinato | | • | • | → | → | → |
| Solo/Duet/Trio/Quartet | | • | • | → | → | → |
| Motive | | • | • | → | → | → |
| Countermelody/Descant | | • | • | → | → | → |
| Augmentation/Diminution | | | • | • | → | → |
| Antiphony | | | • | • | → | → |
| Inversion/Retrograde | | | | • | • | → |
| Hocket | | | | • | • | → |

| | I | II | III | IV | V | VI |
|---|---|---|---|---|---|---|
| Stretto | | | | | • | • |
| Minimalism | | | | | • | • |
| Serial (Twelve-Tone) | | | | | • | • |

| *Compositional Structures* | I | II | III | IV | V | VI |
|---|---|---|---|---|---|---|
| Binary (e.g., AB) | • | • | → | → | → | → |
| Ternary (e.g., ABA) | • | • | → | → | → | → |
| March | • | • | → | → | → | → |
| Canon/Round | • | • | → | → | → | → |
| Waltz | • | • | → | → | → | → |
| Hymn | | • | → | → | → | → |
| Program Music | | • | • | → | → | → |
| Theme and Variation (see page 52) | | • | • | → | → | → |
| Chorale and Chorale Prelude | | • | • | → | → | → |
| Overture | | • | • | → | → | → |
| National Forms (e.g., Polka, Bolero) | | • | • | → | → | → |
| Novelty | | • | • | → | → | → |
| Rondo | | • | • | → | → | → |
| Suite | | • | • | → | → | → |
| Eight-Bar, Twelve-Bar Blues | | • | • | → | → | → |
| Through-Composed/Free | | • | • | → | → | → |
| Aria/Air/Ballad | | • | • | → | → | → |
| Sonata-Allegro | | • | • | → | → | → |
| Fugue | | • | • | → | → | → |
| Fantasy/Fantasia/Rhapsody | | • | • | → | → | → |
| Toccata | | | • | → | → | → |
| Concerto | | | • | • | → | → |
| Chaconne/Passacaglia | | | • | • | → | → |

# Musical Concepts—Timbre/Texture

| *Effects* | I | II | III | IV | V | VI |
|---|---|---|---|---|---|---|
| Muting | | • | • | → | → | → |
| Trill | | • | • | → | → | → |
| Grace Notes | | • | • | → | → | → |
| Flutter Tongue | | | • | • | → | → |
| Echo/Off-Stage | | | • | • | → | → |
| Antiphonal | | | • | • | → | → |
| Jazz Effects (e.g., Fall, Smear) | | | • | • | → | → |
| Vibrato (Diaphragm, Jaw, Hand) | | | • | • | → | → |
| Special Instrumental Techniques (e.g., Buzzing Mouthpiece) | | | • | • | → | → |
| Ornaments (e.g., Mordent, Turn) | | | | • | • | → |

| *Other Concepts Affecting Timbre/Texture* | I | II | III | IV | V | VI |
|---|---|---|---|---|---|---|
| Melody/Accompaniment | • | → | → | → | → | → |
| Orchestration (see page 53) | | • | • | → | → | → |

# Musical Concepts—Expression

| Dynamics | I | II | III | IV | V | VI |
|---|---|---|---|---|---|---|
| mp, mf | • | → | → | → | → | → |
| p, f | • | → | → | → | → | → |
| < >, Crescendo, Decrescendo, Diminuendo | • | • | → | → | → | → |
| pp, ff | | • | → | → | → | → |
| fp | | • | • | → | → | → |
| sfz | | • | • | → | → | → |
| ppp, fff | | | | • | • | → |

| Phrasing | I | II | III | IV | V | VI |
|---|---|---|---|---|---|---|
| Rise, Fall | | • | → | → | → | → |
| Climax | | • | → | → | → | → |
| Cadence | | | • | → | → | → |
| Tension, Release | | | • | • | → | → |
| Silence | | | • | • | → | → |

| Articulation | I | II | III | IV | V | VI |
|---|---|---|---|---|---|---|
| Slur | • | → | → | → | → | → |
| Staccato | • | • | → | → | → | → |
| Accent | • | • | → | → | → | → |
| Legato (see page 54) | • | • | → | → | → | → |
| Marcato | | • | • | → | → | → |
| Portamento | | | • | → | → | → |
| Staccato Slur | | | • | → | → | → |
| Active Release | | | | • | → | → |

| Interpretive Devices | I | II | III | IV | V | VI |
|---|---|---|---|---|---|---|
| Ritardando (Rit.) | • | → | → | → | → | → |
| Accelerando (Accel.) | | • | → | → | → | → |
| Allargando / Rallentando | | • | • | → | → | → |
| Poco a Poco | | • | • | → | → | → |
| Tenuto | | | • | → | → | → |
| Rubato | | | • | → | → | → |
| Con Moto | | | • | → | → | → |
| Più Mosso | | | • | • | → | → |
| Meno Mosso | | | • | • | → | → |
| Stringendo | | | | • | • | → |
| Morendo | | | | • | • | → |

| Stylistic Devices | I | II | III | IV | V | VI |
|---|---|---|---|---|---|---|
| Cantabile | | • | → | → | → | → |
| Maestoso | | • | → | → | → | → |
| Dolce | | • | • | → | → | → |
| Espressivo | | • | • | → | → | → |

| | I | II | III | IV | V | VI |
|---|---|---|---|---|---|---|
| Agitato | | | • | → | → | → |
| Alla Marcia | | | • | → | → | → |
| Animato | | | • | → | → | → |
| Con Spirito | | | • | → | → | → |
| Grandioso | | | • | → | → | → |
| Grazioso | | | • | → | → | → |
| Sostenuto | | | • | → | → | → |
| Appassionato | | | | • | → | → |
| Brilliante | | | | • | → | → |
| Pesante | | | | • | → | → |
| Leggiero | | | | • | → | → |
| Tranquillo | | | | • | → | → |
| Furioso | | | | • | • | → |
| A Piacere | | | | • | • | → |
| Scherzando | | | | • | • | → |
| Semplice | | | | • | • | → |
| Giocoso | | | | | • | → |
| Martellato | | | | | • | → |

# Historical Information

| *Periods of Music* | I | II | III | IV | V | VI |
|---|---|---|---|---|---|---|
| Classical | | • | • | → | → | → |
| Baroque | | • | • | → | → | → |
| Renaissance | | • | • | → | → | → |
| Romantic | | • | • | → | → | → |
| Impressionistic | | | • | • | → | → |
| Twentieth Century | | | • | • | → | → |

| *Ethnic Music* | I | II | III | IV | V | VI |
|---|---|---|---|---|---|---|
| Latin | | • | → | → | → | → |
| Mexican | | • | → | → | → | → |
| Italian | | • | → | → | → | → |
| English | | • | → | → | → | → |
| French | | • | → | → | → | → |
| German | | • | → | → | → | → |
| Jewish | | • | → | → | → | → |
| African | | | • | → | → | → |
| American Indian | | | • | → | → | → |
| Asian | | | • | → | → | → |
| Slavic | | | • | → | → | → |

| *Music Technology* | I | II | III | IV | V | VI |
|---|---|---|---|---|---|---|
| Electronic/Computer—MIDI | | | • | → | → | → |
| Wind Instrument Development | | | • | • | → | → |
| Multi-Media (e.g., Laser) | | | | | • | → |

| Composers | I | II | III | IV | V | VI |
|---|---|---|---|---|---|---|
| "Classical" | | • | → | → | → | → |
| John Philip Sousa (see page 57) | | • | → | → | → | → |
| Henry Fillmore | | • | → | → | → | → |
| Karl King | | • | → | → | → | → |
| Edwin Franco Goldman | | • | → | → | → | → |
| Other Composers of Marches | | • | • | → | → | → |
| Gustav Holst | | | • | → | → | → |
| Ralph Vaughan Williams | | | • | → | → | → |
| Percy Grainger | | | • | → | → | → |
| Other English Composers | | | • | → | → | → |
| Clifton Williams | | | • | → | → | → |
| Alfred Reed | | | • | → | → | → |
| Other American Composers | | | • | → | → | → |
| Vaclav Nehlybel | | | • | → | → | → |
| Howard Hanson | | | | • | → | → |
| William Schuman | | | | • | → | → |
| Robert Russell Bennett | | | | • | → | → |
| Vincent Persichetti | | | | • | → | → |

| Conductors | I | II | III | IV | V | VI |
|---|---|---|---|---|---|---|
| John Philip Sousa | | • | → | → | → | → |
| Patrick Gilmore | | | • | → | → | → |
| Edwin Franco Goldman | | | • | → | → | → |
| Frederick Fennell | | | • | → | → | → |
| William Revelli | | | • | → | → | → |
| John Paynter | | | • | → | → | → |
| Mark Hindsley | | | | • | → | → |
| Walter Beeler | | | | • | → | → |

| Instrumentalists | I | II | III | IV | V | VI |
|---|---|---|---|---|---|---|
| James Galway/Flute | | | • | → | → | → |
| Jean-Pierre Rampal/Flute | | | • | → | → | → |
| Heinz Holliger/Oboe | | | • | → | → | → |
| John Mack/Oboe | | | • | → | → | → |
| Stanley Drucker/Clarinet | | | • | → | → | → |
| Anthony Gigliotti/Clarinet | | | • | → | → | → |
| Richard Stoltzman/Clarinet | | | • | → | → | → |
| Bernard Garfield/Bassoon | | | • | → | → | → |
| Milan Turkovic/Bassoon | | | • | → | → | → |
| Branford Marsalis/Saxophone | | | • | → | → | → |
| Sigurd Rascher/Saxophone | | | • | → | → | → |
| Eugene Rousseau/Saxophone | | | • | → | → | → |
| Donald Sinta/Saxophone | | | • | → | → | → |
| Dennis Brain/French Horn | | | • | → | → | → |
| Dale Clevenger/French Horn | | | • | → | → | → |
| Philip Farkas/French Horn | | | • | → | → | → |

| | | | | | | |
|---|---|---|---|---|---|---|
| Herbert L. Clarke/Cornet | | | | • | → | → | → |
| Adolph Herseth/Trumpet | | | | • | → | → | → |
| Wynton Marsalis/Trumpet | | | | • | → | → | → |
| Arthur Pryor/Trombone | | | | • | → | → | → |
| Brian Bowman/Euphonium | | | | • | → | → | → |
| Leonard Falcone/Euphonium | | | | • | → | → | → |
| Arnold Jacobs/Tuba | | | | • | → | → | → |
| Harvey Phillips/Tuba | | | | • | → | → | → |
| Haskell Harr/Snare Drum | | | | • | → | → | → |
| Gordon Stout/Snare Drum | | | | • | → | → | → |

| *Styles* | I | II | III | IV | V | VI |
|---|---|---|---|---|---|---|
| Folk | • | → | → | → | → | → |
| March | • | → | → | → | → | → |
| Dance (e.g., Ballet, Folk) | • | → | → | → | → | → |
| Country | • | → | → | → | → | → |
| Hymn | • | → | → | → | → | → |
| Jazz | | • | → | → | → | → |

| *Performance Practice* | I | II | III | IV | V | VI |
|---|---|---|---|---|---|---|
| Interpretation (e.g., Characteristic Style, Tempo) | • | • | → | → | → | → |
| Ornamentation | | • | → | → | → |
| Instrumentation | | | | • | → | → |

# Creativity and Valuing Concepts

| *Creating Music* | I | II | III | IV | V | VI |
|---|---|---|---|---|---|---|
| Composing | | • | • | → | → | → |
| Arranging | | | | • | → | → |

| *Improvisation* | I | II | III | IV | V | VI |
|---|---|---|---|---|---|---|
| Free | | • | → | → | → | → |
| Jazz | | • | • | → | → | → |
| Solo/Cadenza (see page 61) | | | • | → | → | → |
| Aleatoric | | | | • | • | → |

| *Phrasing/Line* | I | II | III | IV | V | VI |
|---|---|---|---|---|---|---|
| Intensity | | • | → | → | → | → |
| Nuance, Inflection, Subtlety | | • | • | → | → | → |

| *Expression/Emotion* | I | II | III | IV | V | VI |
|---|---|---|---|---|---|---|
| Happy | | • | • | → | → | → |
| Angry/Aggressive/Violent | | • | • | → | → | → |
| Calm/Gentle/Peaceful | | • | • | → | → | → |

| *Valuing* | I | II | III | IV | V | VI |
|---|---|---|---|---|---|---|
| Critical Thinking (Evaluation/Analyzing) | • | → | → | → | → | → |
| Discrimination (see page 62) | • | • | → | → | → | → |
| Aesthetic Response | • | • | → | → | → | → |

# Sample Activities
## and Materials

# Individual Performance
## and Listening Skills

# Basic Wind Instrument Skills

These skills are common to all wind instruments. They should be introduced during Level I instruction and should be continually reinforced throughout instrumental music study. While it is ideal to introduce these concepts in homogeneous groupings, commonalities among the skills make them quite accessible in heterogeneous settings, the only difficulties being with differences in various fingerings and hand positions. However, once a step-by-step procedure is established, these too can be taught in heterogeneous settings.

One should always remember that these skills are *basic* to quality wind instrument performance. They should *not* be neglected or forgotten as more advanced skills are introduced. Continual reinforcement of these skills is the key to future success. For a complete listing of the basic wind instrument skills, see the *Skills and Concepts—Recommended Performance Levels* section. A sample of a teaching plan for a basic instrument skill follows.

# Basic Wind Instrument Skills

## Specific Skill or Concept: *Breathing*
## Performance Level: *I*

### Suggested Activities or Strategies

| Instructional Sequence | Techniques/Devices | Checks |
| --- | --- | --- |
| *The students should:* | | |
| 1. Empty lungs. | | |
| 2. Breathe in while teacher counts to four. | | 2. Make sure students expand beltlines, keeping shoulders down. |
| 3. Take three more "sips" of breath. | | |
| 4. Hiss air out while teacher counts; memorize the count on which they run out of breath. | 4. a. Count at a moderate, not slow, tempo. | 4. a. Encourage students to hiss for a greater number of counts each time the exercise is done. |
| | b. Encourage individual improvement, not competition between individuals. | b. The first time through the exercise, students should stand when they run out of breath. The second time, have students remain standing to start, then sit when they run out of breath. |
| | | c. Point out that body size does not necessarily relate to breath capacity. |
| | | d. Have students record the date and their counts occasionally, maybe in front of band method book, to chart improvement. |

### Suggested Materials

**Texts or Methods**

*The Art of Brass Playing*, P. Farkas

# Advanced Wind Instrument Skills

Advanced wind instrument skills are complex and only applicable to selected instruments; therefore, teaching of these skills in heterogenous groupings would be quite difficult. While it would be ideal for students to learn these skills in private lessons, private instruction is not always available to public school music students. It then becomes incumbent upon the instrumental music teacher to ensure that students are at least exposed to Level III/IV advanced skills and possibly to the higher-level skills. For a complete list of the advanced wind instrument skills, see the *Skills and Concepts—Recommended Performance Levels* section. A sample plan for teaching an advanced wind instrument skill follows.

# Advanced Wind Instrument Skills

## Specific Skill or Concept: *Transposition*
## Performance Level: *III / IV*

## Suggested Activities or Strategies

| Instructional Sequence | Techniques/Devices | Checks |
|---|---|---|
| **1.** Ask students, "What would we do if we were asked to play backup for (any famous rock, pop, or classical singer that the students relate to), but that singer couldn't sing in the range required in our arrangement?" Student suggestions may include rewriting, but should lead to a discussion of transposition. | | |
| **2.** Choose a simple tune and have students transpose it mentally by changing its key signature. | **2.** For example, if the key is B♭, have them play in B; if the key is G, have them play in G♭; if the key is E♭, have them play in E. | **2. a.** Check with each section to see if students understand the new key signature. Ask students to practice the new scale once or twice.<br><br>**b.** Tape record the original tune; then record the transposed tune. |
| **3. a.** Using the same tune, instruct everyone to play in the key that is one whole step up, such as from E♭ to F. | **3.** Start with the last two measures, or even just the final chord. Work backward through the piece for awhile, adding one or two measures at a time. | **3. a.** Check that each section knows the target key signature. |
| **b.** Do the same exercise, but have students move the key a whole step down, such as from E♭ to D♭. | | **b.** Tape record. |
| **4. a.** Give students a unison four- or eight-bar melody and ask each student to write out a further transposition a perfect fourth up or down; then play it. | | **4.** Tape record. |
| **b.** Have students try transposing the same melody by sight, with the written transposition hidden. | | |
| **5.** Point out the potential for abrupt transpositions; then try one at a preplanned number in the piece. | | **5.** Tape record. |

## Suggested Materials

### Texts or Methods

*Band Today*, Book III, J. Ployhar

# Specific Instrument Skills

Individual skills applicable to each instrument are contained in this section. Several skills are common to all instruments but are explained in detail because of great differences in the instructional approach. Again, because differences exist between instruments, teaching these skills in heterogeneous groupings is extremely difficult. However, if a step-by-step sequential approach is used, many of the common skills can be taught effectively in heterogeneous groups.

As with the advanced instrument skills, one should not neglect higher-level skills simply because private instruction may not be possible. The teacher should make every effort possible to include these as part of the students' basic instrumental music education.

For a complete listing of specific instrument skills to be introduced, see the *Skills and Concepts—Recommended Performance Levels* section. The following are examples of teaching plans for specific instrument skills.

# Specific Flute/Piccolo Skills

## Specific Skill or Concept: *Assembly*
## Performance Level: *I*

## Suggested Activities or Strategies

| Instructional Sequence | Techniques/Devices | Checks |
| --- | --- | --- |
| *The student should:* | | |
| **1.** Study the placement of the flute sections in the case. | **1.** Model the process of assembling the flute for the student while giving verbal instructions. | |
| **2.** Identify the head joint (with embouchure plate), middle joint (longest section), and foot joint. | | |
| **3.** Take the middle joint out of the case by grasping the area engraved with the brand name. | | **3.** Make sure the student does not grasp the flute over key and rod mechanisms. |
| **4.** Take the head joint out of the case with the other hand. Insert the open end of the head joint into the engraved end of the middle joint with a twisting motion. | | **4.** Make sure the student inserts head joint straight into the middle joint, not at an angle. |
| **5.** Align the embouchure hole with the row of large keys on the top of the middle joint. | **5.** Some manufacturers place lightly scratched alignment marks at this joint. | |
| **6.** Take the foot joint from the case by grasping the end below the key and rod mechanisms. Twist the open end of the foot joint onto the open end of the middle joint. | | **6.** Make sure the student twists the foot joint straight onto the middle joint, not at an angle. |
| **7.** Align the rod of the foot joint with the center of the large keys on the middle joint. | **7.** Have the student draw an imaginary straight line from the embouchure hole, across the long row of keys (middle joint), and down the rod of the foot joint. | |

## Suggested Materials

### Texts or Methods

*The Art of Flute Playing,* E. Putnik, 6.
*Guide to Teaching Woodwinds,* F. Westphal, 14–16.

# Specific Oboe Skills

## Specific Skill or Concept: *Care and Maintenance*
## Performance Level: *I*

### Suggested Activities or Strategies

| Instructional Sequence | Techniques/Devices | Checks |
| --- | --- | --- |
| *The student should:* | *The student should:* | |
| **1.** Check that the oboe has been carefully cleaned after each playing experience. | **1.** Use a clean turkey or pheasant feather or a cloth swab with nylon string and a weight. | **1.** Make sure the student is careful when using a cloth swab. Some swabs will *not* go through the top joint. |
| **2.** Remove moisture from the reed before storing it. | **2.** Store reeds in a proper reed case. | **2.** Make sure the student remembers where the reed is at all times when playing. The reed is easily broken through carelessness. |
| **3.** Keep instrument from extreme temperature changes. | **3.** If the instrument is cold, warm it up by placing both joints under arms near the armpits. | **3.** Make sure students use a humidor in dry climates (only for wooden instruments). |
| **4.** Oil the keys every three to four months. | **4.** Use only top-quality key oil designed for woodwind instruments. | |

### Suggested Materials

#### Texts or Methods

*The Art of Oboe Playing*, R. Sprenkle and D. Ledet
*The Oboe Revealed*, C. Sawicki

# Specific Clarinet Skills

## Specific Skill or Concept: *Crossing the Break*
## Performance Level: *I / II*

*Note: Facility in crossing the break depends on a solid embouchure, full tone production, and finger strength and control. These skills should be well established before attempting the clarion register and crossing the break.*

## Suggested Activities or Strategies

| Instructional Sequence | Techniques/Devices | Checks |
|---|---|---|
| *Finger strength and control:* | | |
| 1. With no reed or ligature, and with the bell in the student's lap and the clarinet resting on the student's left shoulder, have students put thumbs in place. | | ■ Make sure the clarinet is in good repair. |
| | | ■ Check reed strength—it should be at least medium hard. |
|    a. Student should go down the clarinet *slowly,* one finger at a time. | 1. a. Have students press fingers down hard, spreading out the "fat" of each finger. | ■ Be sure sufficient mouthpiece is in student's mouth to allow for maximum reed vibration on the "V." |
|    b. Instruct student to cover the holes completely and to keep the fingers rounded and close to the clarinet. | | ■ Check student's head position and angle of clarinet mouthpiece. |
|    c. Student should raise one finger at a time, *slowly.* | | ■ Check for flat chin. |
| 2. Student should add little fingers on the low F and E keys to establish the pattern. | | ■ Always insist on a full clarinet sound. |
| 3. When the above exercise is mastered, allow the student to blow on the clarinet while executing the finger exercise. When a note squeaks or doesn't speak, student should go immediately back to the top (or bottom) and start again. | | ■ Check hand positions, especially for position of the thumbs. |
| | | ■ Make sure students keep fingers close to tone holes while playing both ascending and descending notes. |
| 4. Develop this exercise into a rhythmic F major scale. | 4. Do not rush through the *chalumeau* register. Develop extra songs utilizing these notes. Do not ask students to attempt the clarion register until the *chalumeau* register is solid. | |
| 5. Test the student's embouchure and tone production by pressing the register key while the student plays low A or B♭. | 5. Let the low note settle itself first. Press the register key at unexpected rhythmic intervals to force the student to keep an appropriate embouchure at all times. If the low note isn't solid, the high note won't speak. | 5. In general, students will need to blow a little harder and the embouchure will need to be a little firmer than they are accustomed to. |

Crossing the Break *(continued)*

| Instructional Sequence | Techniques/Devices | Checks |
| --- | --- | --- |

*Finger strength and control:*

**6.** Show student how to use the register key emphasizing a slight rolling action of the thumb, with fingers solid on the keys and no change in embouchure.

**7.** Use the F major scale, playing four beats on each scale tone and using the register key to play a higher note for four beats.

**8.** Have students make the transition to the C major scale (starting on the third space).

**9.** Teach the tuning scale (starting on low C) using the right-hand down technique for throat tones. Reinforce this technique whenever possible in band music and method books.

## Suggested Materials

**Texts or Methods**

*Best in Class,* Book 1, B. Pearson, 21–22.
*Sessions in Sound,* B. Buehlman and K. Whitcomb, 20–21.
*Building Tomorrow's Band ... Today!* Book 1, J. Burden, 24.
*Yamaha Band Student,* Book 1, S. Feldstein and J. O'Reilly, 25–27.
*Music for Young Woodwinds, Our First Clarinet Book,* H. Van Lijnschooten, 18, 20, 24, 25, 27, 34.
*Alfred's Basic Band Method,* Book 1, S. Feldstein and J. O'Reilly, 26, 28, 30.
*Alfred's New Band Method,* Book 1, S. Feldstein, 22, 24, 26.
*Clarinet Student,* Level 1, F. Weber and R. Lowry, 14, 16, 17, 21.
*First Division Band Method,* Part 1, F. Weber, 18, 22.
*First Division Band Method,* Part 2, F. Weber, 9, 25, 28.
*The Beacon Band Method,* Book 1, H. Bennett, 22, 23.
*Advanced Rubank Method,* Vol. 1, H. Voxman and W. Gower, 58, 59.
*Visual Band Method,* Book 1, V. Leidig and L. Niehaus, 24, 26–28.

# Specific Bassoon Skills

## Specific Skill or Concept: *Reed Adjustment*
## Performance Level: *II / III*

## Suggested Activities or Strategies

| Instructional Sequence | Techniques/Devices | Checks |
|---|---|---|
| *Reed problem:* | | |
| **1.** Poor tone production. | **1.** With a rounded plaque inside the reed to support the blades, rub the blades with fingertips to introduce pore-filling dirt. | |
| **2.** Reed is too stiff. | **2. a.** Reduce the arch and tip opening with a pliers at the first wire. | |
| | **b.** Scrape or file from the back to the tip in one direction. | **2. b.** Reed should be able to "crow." |
| **3.** Reed has unevenly balanced blades. | **3.** Check for balance by holding the soaked reed in front of a light source. | **3.** The opaqueness of the reed should be even on both sides. |
| **4.** Reed tongues poorly: | | |
| **a.** Uneven attack from low F to B♭. | **4. a.** The tip opening is too narrow and can be expanded by squeezing the reed from top to bottom with a pliers at the first wire. | **4. a.** The low range should be responsive. |
| **b.** Other ranges are sluggish. | **b.** Work down the area just behind the tip with a file. The center of the tip should be thicker than the corners. | **b.** The upper ranges should be responsive. |
| **5.** Reed is too thin or flat in pitch: | | |
| **a.** Reed becomes water-logged. | **5. a.** Let the reed sit for a period to dry out. | |
| **b.** Reed is flat in pitch. | **b.** Reed is too thin at the tip. Clip off about 1/64" from the tip, or squeeze the reed at the sides by the second wire. | **5. b.** Third space E should be in tune. |

## Suggested Materials

### Texts or Methods

*The Art of Bassoon Playing,* W. Spencer, 34, 36, 37.

# Specific Saxophone Skills

## Specific Skill or Concept: *Instrument Position*
## Performance Level: *I*

## Suggested Activities or Strategies

| Instructional Sequence | Techniques/Devices | Checks |
| --- | --- | --- |
| *The student should:* | | |
| **1.** Sit with feet flat on floor, back straight and away from chair. | **1.** Student should sit up tall. | **1.** Student's feet should be flat on the floor. |
| **2.** Keep arms away from body. | **2.** Students should keep "wings up," not parallel to floor. | **2.** Student's elbows should not rest on thighs. |
| **3.** Adjust the neck strap to the correct length. | **3.** Have student let go, teacher grasps saxophone bell. Mouthpiece should go to student's mouth. | **3.** Neck strap, rather than hands, should support the instrument. The sax should not rest on chair. |
| **4.** Place saxophone forward at middle of upper leg. | **4.** Student should look ahead, not toward floor. | **4.** Make sure you can see student's eyes. |
| **5.** Turn mouthpiece so head is straight (saxophone may be at slight angle). | | |
| **6.** If holding saxophone in front, follow same steps. | | **6.** Saxophone should not rest on chair and arms should not rest on legs. If arms aren't free, place the saxophone on student's side. |

## Suggested Materials

### Texts or Methods

*Practical Hints on Playing the Saxophone,* E. Rousseau, 5, 6.
*Art of Saxophone Playing,* L. Teal, 30, 31.
*Guide to Teaching Woodwinds,* F. Westphal, 124–36.

# Specific French Horn Skills

## Specific Skill or Concept: *Stopping*
## Performance Level: *IV*

## Suggested Activities or Strategies

| Instructional Sequence | Techniques/Devices | Checks |
|---|---|---|

*In stopping, the hand does not stuff the bell; it stops the bell.*
*Have students follow this technique:*

**1.** The palm of the right hand closes the bell by pressing firmly against the side of the bell.

**2.** The tops of the fingertips will push with equal pressure against the opposite side of the bell. The image of sealing or stopping is very important here.

**3.** There should be absolutely no space between fingers or between the sides of the hand and the bell surface.

**4.** Push a very steady stream of air through the horn to produce a stopped quality.

**5.** All pitches (once stopped) must be read and fingered 1/2 step lower using the F side of the horn exclusively.

■ Demonstration is essential both to see the hand position and to hear the quality of the stopped tone.

■ Practice open compared to stopped. For example, play G open and then G stopped (fingered as an F#). Work for speed and fluency in the change. Start in the upper middle range. Stopped horn is very difficult in the lower range. Second line G and above would be appropriate.

■ Practice long tones with very controlled and powerful crescendos. This exercise should develop the brassy quality characteristic of stopped horn.

■ The symbols used are:

    stopped +

    open   o

■ Hand position must be correct before a student can be expected to master stopped horn technique.

■ If the student cannot master the stopping motions and resorts to stuffing, his or her hand may still be too small for this technique.

■ If the tone is a muffled and distant sound instead of the brassy quality, the student is not using enough air with an adequate amount of support. Go back to long tones.

■ Stopped horn demands a very intense air stream or pitches will be very sharp.

■ Stopped horn should be practiced with a tuner at all times.

## Suggested Materials

### Texts or Methods

*The Art of French Horn Playing*, P. Farkas
*A Creative Approach to the French Horn*, H. Berv

### Music

"Villanelle," Dukas, Level IV
"Fantasy for Horn," Arnold, Level IV
"Morceau de Concert Op. 94," Saint Säens, Level IV

# Specific Cornet/Trumpet Skills

## Specific Skill or Concept: *Instrument Position*
## Performance Level: *I*

### Suggested Activities or Strategies

| Instructional Sequence | Techniques/Devices | Checks |
|---|---|---|
| *The student should:* | | |
| **1.** Hold the instrument with the left hand around the valve casing, with four fingers on the bell side, the thumb on the mouthpiece side, and the ring finger in the finger ring. | **1.** Student should put out the left hand as if in a handshake, and grab the instrument around the valve casing. | **1.** Adjust the left hand finger ring so the left ring finger moves it easily. |
| **2.** Place the right thumb in the space between the first and second valves with the right index finger on the first valve, the middle finger on the second, and the ring finger on the third. The right-hand little finger should rest *on top* of the right-hand finger ring. | **2.** Student should make a backwards "c" with the right hand thumb and fingers. | **2.** The *tips* of the student's fingers should rest on the valve caps. |
| | **3.** Show student a picture or diagram of the proper playing position. | **3.** The little finger on the right hand should *not* be in the finger ring. |
| | **4.** Demonstrate the proper position to student. | **4.** The right thumb should be *straight*. |
| | | **5.** Bell should point out, and only slightly downward. |

### Suggested Materials

#### Texts or Methods

*Band Plus,* Book 1, J. Swearingen and B. Buehlman
*Band Today,* Book I, J. Ployhar
*Learning Unlimited,* Book I, A. Jenson

# Specific Trombone Skills

## Specific Skill or Concept: *Legato Tonguing*
## Performance Level: *II / III*

### Suggested Activities or Strategies

| Instructional Sequence | Techniques/Devices | Checks |
|---|---|---|
| **1.** Instruct student that legato slurring on trombone is not the same as on other brass instruments. | **1.** Demonstrate the trombone legato tongue by:<br><br>   **a.** tonguing the first note of a slur with *too* syllable.<br><br>   **b.** tonguing the next notes with *doo* syllable.<br><br>   **c.** moving slide quickly. | **1.** Watch to see that student moves slide quickly and smoothly. |
| **2.** Practice by repetition. | **2.** Ask student to match teacher's slur.<br><br>**3.** Student should practice slur using exercises provided in beginning band method book. | **2.** Listen to make sure that tongue does not get involved with legato notes.<br><br>**3.** Listen for a possible glissando. |

### Suggested Materials

**Texts or Methods**

*Best in Class,* Books 1 and 2, B. Pearson
*Melodious Etudes for Trombone,* M. Bordagni and J. Rochut
*The Art of Trombone Playing,* E. Kleinhammer

# Specific Baritone/Euphonium Skills

## Specific Skill or Concept: *Vibrato*
## Performance Level: *III*

### Suggested Activities or Strategies

| Instructional Sequence | Techniques/Devices | Checks |
|---|---|---|
| *The student should:* | | |
| **1.** Begin with a good tone. | ■ The student must be able to control the pulsations. | ■ Vibrato must be under control. |
| **2.** Fluctuate pitch with jaw/lip, pulse per beat ♩=60. | ■ Higher notes use quicker pulses than lower notes. | ■ Vibrato adds warmth to a good tone; it does not improve a poor tone. |
| **3.** Gradually increase rhythmic pulse ♫ \| ♪♪♪ \| ♫♫ \| ♫♫♫ \| etc. | ■ The student should sing passage, possibly adding words. | |
| **4.** Gradually increase metronome tempo. | ■ Then imitate on instrument. | |
| **5.** Listen to recordings of solo euphonium performance. | | |

### Suggested Materials

**Texts or Methods**

*Melodious Etudes for Trombone*, M. Bordagni and J. Rochut

# Specific Tuba/Sousaphone Skills

Specific Skill or Concept: *Fourth-Valve Technique*
Performance Level: *III / IV*

## Suggested Activities or Strategies

| Instructional Sequence | Techniques/Devices | Checks |
|---|---|---|
| **1.** Begin as soon as student's hands can manage fourth valve (and as soon as an instrument is available). | ■ Approach fourth valve from intonation standpoint. | ■ Watch hand position especially with fingerings that combine the fourth valve with the other three. |
| **2.** Introduce low C fourth valve instead of valves one and three. Have the student play the note each way and listen for the difference. | | |
| **3.** Include low B natural with valves two and four. | | |
| **4.** Begin teaching lower register by introducing the possibility of a two-octave E♭ scale. | | |

## Suggested Materials

### Texts or Methods

*Brass Anthology,* 263, 264.

# Specific Snare Drum Skills

## Specific Skill or Concept: *Paradiddle*
## Performance Level: *I*

### Suggested Activities or Strategies

| Instructional Sequence | Techniques/Devices | Checks |
| --- | --- | --- |
| *The student should:* | | |
| **1.** Start with alternating, even, single strokes. Switch to paradiddles without interrupting the flow, then back into single strokes. Use a metronome! | **1.** The paradiddle consists of two single strokes followed by a double stroke. The pattern, if repeated, is usually played in an alternating sticking pattern. Ex.: | **1.** All patterns should be played evenly with a consistent sound in both hands and with rhythmic accuracy. |
| | R  L  R  R    L  R  L  L | |
| **2.** Start with even double strokes. Without interrupting the rhythm, switch to paradiddles and then back into double strokes. | **2.** This rudiment is traditionally played with an accent on the first beat of each four-note pattern. In contemporary music, this rudiment may appear with accents on any note of the pattern. The pattern also may start on the second, third, or fourth note of the paradiddle. | **2.** When played correctly, the sticking patterns played should be discernible from each other. |
| **3.** Practice playing alternating paradiddles while shifting accents to different beats. | | |
| **4.** Practice playing alternating paradiddles beginning on the second, third, or fourth note of the paradiddle. Ex.: | | |
| ‖: LRR/L   RLL/R :‖ | | |

### Suggested Materials

#### Texts or Methods

*Intermediate Drum Method,* R. Burns and S. Feldstein, 3, 9–12, 34–35.
*Modern Rudimental Swing Solos,* C. Wilcoxon, 5, 17, 45.
*Stick Control,* G. Stone
*Master Studies,* J. Morello

#### Music

This rudiment can be practiced in music containing passages with straight eighth notes or straight sixteenths.

# Ensemble Performance
## and Listening Skills

# Ensemble Performance and Listening Skills

These skills, while taught as individual instrumental skills, must also be presented in the context of ensemble skills. They should be introduced as early in the learning process as possible and continually reinforced throughout instrumental music study. All too often, ensemble skills are relegated to a status secondary to specific instrumental technical skills, are not introduced at the beginning of the ensemble experience, or are briefly mentioned prior to a performance. Continued emphasis on these skills is the only way they can become second nature to the student. For a complete listing of ensemble performance and listening skills to be introduced, see the *Skills and Concepts—Recommended Performance Levels* section. A sample plan for teaching an ensemble listening skill follows.

# Ensemble Skills

## Specific Skill or Concept: *Listening*
## Performance Level: *I*

## Suggested Activities or Strategies

| Instructional Sequence | Techniques/Devices | Checks |
|---|---|---|
| **1.** Explain importance of ensemble listening. Use the analogy of a team in which each member has a different role to play, but each member is equally important. | **1.** Play a recording of an instrumental piece and ask students to identify features as piece progresses. For example, ask students what instrument is playing the melody at certain times. | |
| **2.** Choose a simple two- or three-part round that everyone knows how to sing. | **2.** Ask students to sing together then in parts to practice independence. | |
| **3.** Ask students to play the same round in order to give additional practice at independent playing. | **3.** Ask students to play the round together, then in parts. | **3.** Listen for mistakes caused by a student playing someone else's part. |
| **4.** Reinforce with additional practice. | **4.** When students can play the round easily, ask them to listen for other parts as they play their own to hear the variety and texture created. | |

## Suggested Materials

### Texts or Methods

*The Creative Director: Alternative Rehearsal Techniques,* E. Lisk

# Musical Concepts

# Musical Concepts

The musical elements of rhythm, melody, harmony, form, timbre and texture, and expression form the conceptual basis for this document. These elements, with their respective concepts, contain the myriad of terms, notations, structures, and devices commonly found in a comprehensive band curriculum. Specific elements were used to provide a logical means to categorize the items and also to provide a curricular basis for teaching these items.

The majority of these concepts must be introduced during Level I instruction. However, many of the individual concepts may be combined within elements or combined with concepts from other elements. As an experienced educator knows, many elements of this conceptual learning take place simultaneously with other elements.

The higher-level concepts should not be ignored. While some may seem out of reach for a basic curriculum, educators should strive continually to expand their curriculum to include these items. Continued reinforcement of previously learned concepts is the key to success. Teachers must remember that simply teaching a musical concept once is not sufficient for effective learning.

For a complete listing of musical concepts to be introduced, see the *Skills and Concepts—Recommended Performance Levels* section. A sampling of activities for teaching music concepts appears on the following pages.

# Rhythm—Time Signature and Rhythmic Notations

**Specific Skill or Concept:** $\frac{2}{4}$. $\frac{3}{4}$. $\frac{4}{4}$. *(fast* $\frac{6}{8}$, $\frac{9}{8}$, $\frac{12}{8}$ *)* ♩. ♩ ♫♩ ♩♪ ♩.. ♩.♫♩

**Performance Level:** *II*

## Suggested Activites or Strategies

| Instructional Sequence | Techniques/Devices | Checks |
| --- | --- | --- |
| **1.** Review the difference between "beats" and "counts." | **1. a.** Conduct a beat pattern in slow $\frac{3}{4}$ time; have the students count and tap their toes as you conduct.<br><br>**b.** Conduct a beat pattern in fast $\frac{3}{4}$ time (one to a bar); have the students count and tap their toes as you conduct. | **1.** Make certain that all students know that "beats" refers to toe tapping or conducting; "counts" may refer to the beat or just to the mathematical value of the notes. |
| **2.** Review slow $\frac{3}{8}$ and $\frac{6}{8}$ time signatures and beats. | **2.** Discuss what kinds of notes get one count, two counts, three counts, and six counts. | **2.** Question individuals to check general understanding; draw the note values on the blackboard or overhead projector and have students signal with the correct number of fingers as you point to each note's value in random. |
| **3.** Introduce the concept of one beat per dotted quarter. | **3.** Start the students counting and tapping in $\frac{6}{8}$ time at a moderately slow speed as you conduct; gradually speed up until everyone has stopped tapping. Or choose a slow speed, then a moderately fast speed, then a fast speed, and have students try to count and tap. | **3.** Scan the class to be sure of full participation; encourage students with less coordination by guiding foot. |
| **4.** Introduce fast $\frac{6}{8}$ time. | **4. a.** Explain that when the tempo in $\frac{6}{8}$ time is so fast that we can no longer tap every count, we tap only on the strong counts of every measure.<br><br>**b.** Conduct and count fast $\frac{6}{8}$ time; encourage students to discover what counts coincide with the beat.<br><br>**c.** Explain that sometimes we count only the strong beats, in which case the count note becomes the dotted quarter. | **4.** Emphasize counts one and four in your conducting and counting. Scan the class for participation. |
| **5.** Introduce common rhythms in fast $\frac{6}{8}$ time. | **5. a.** Begin with ♩. ♩. and proceed with<br><br>♫♫\|♫♫\|♩ ♪ ♩ ♪\|<br>♫♩ ♩♪\|♩ ♪ ♫♩\|♩. \| | **5. a.** Teacher can clap, students respond; teacher points to rhythm, students respond. Constantly monitor for participation and walk among students if |

$\frac{2}{8}$  $\frac{3}{8}$  $\frac{4}{8}$  (fast $\frac{6}{8}$, $\frac{9}{8}$, $\frac{12}{8}$ ) *(continued)*

| Instructional Sequence | Techniques/Devices | Checks |
| --- | --- | --- |
| | Teach first by rote (feeling); then emphasize notation: write the various rhythms on the board or overhead in random order. Point to the various rhythms as students tap and count out loud, either by six counts or two, whichever you prefer. If you use a two count, you must decide what syllables to use to describe the subdivision, such as 1-la-li, 2-la-li or 1-&-a, 2-&-a, and how you want the rhythm ♩ ♪ vocalized. | possible to encourage focus on the activity. |
| | **b.** Explain and demonstrate how eighth and quarter rests affect fast $\frac{6}{8}$ rhythms. Ex.: | **b.** Emphasize how rests change the style and looks of the music, but do little to change the "feel" of the music. Use selected exercises from the text to check understanding. |
| | **c.** Using exercises printed in the method book or on an overhead transparency, have volunteers attempt to count and clap, tap and count, or otherwise perform the selected rhythms. After a correction has been made, have the whole class perform. | **c.** Offering a reward of a sticker or points to the first student to do a difficult rhythm correctly may inspire more children to attempt the rhythms. |
| **6.** Introduce the concept of fast $\frac{3}{8}$ time. | **6. a.** Count and conduct in fast $\frac{3}{8}$ time and encourage students to imitate. | **6.** Walk among students and make them focus on the sound. Monitor for attention and maintain discipline or make corrections by touching or signalling. |
| | **b.** Use exercises in the method book to check understanding. | |
| **7.** Introduce the concept of $\frac{9}{8}$ and $\frac{12}{8}$ time signatures based on their counting of fast $\frac{6}{8}$ time. | **7.** Use exercises printed in method book and emphasize relationship to counting fast $\frac{6}{8}$ and $\frac{3}{8}$ time. Introduce new rhythms such as o· by example and performance. | **7.** Ask students to point to the rhythm in their book that gets so many counts or sounds like a rhythm you perform. Walk among students to check individual understanding. After the student learning has had time to become firm, you can give a playing/performance test, either individually or by small group. |
| **8.** Introduce sixteenth note subdivision within the $\frac{6}{8}$ context. | **8.** Demonstrate how eighth notes in compound meters subdivide to produce more complex rhythms. Use blackboard or overhead projector to show examples. | **8.** Ask a few pertinent questions of selected individuals to check understanding. |

$\overset{2}{\phantom{p}}$ $\overset{3}{\phantom{p}}$ $\overset{4}{\phantom{p}}$ (fast $\frac{6}{8}$, $\frac{9}{8}$, $\frac{12}{8}$ ) *(continued)*

| Instructional Sequence | Techniques/Devices | Checks |
|---|---|---|
| **9. a.** Introduce common sixteenth note rhythms in $\frac{6}{8}$ context and encourage transfer of rhythms to other compound meters. | **9. a.** Teach by rote the following rhythms in fast $\frac{6}{8}$ (for example, teacher claps or speaks rhythm, students imitate): **b.** Introduce notation for sixteenth note rhythms on board or overhead. **c.** Using exercises printed in a method book, on an overhead sheet, or in a piece of band music, have volunteers attempt to count and clap, count and tap, or otherwise perform the selected rhythms. After a correction has been made, have the whole class perform. **d.** Learn and perform music that uses all of these concepts. | **9. a.** Teacher can clap, students respond; teacher points to rhythm, students respond. Constantly monitor for participation and walk among students if possible to encourage focus on the activity. **b.** Review basic mathematical relationships of notes with students. **c.** Precision of performance should be a goal that is more and more valued by the teacher. Encourage students to listen and become one unit even as they speak or clap but especially as they play together. **d.** Record rehearsals and performances and evaluate. Each day, ask individual sections to perform difficult rhythms precisely. |

## Suggested Materials

### Texts or Methods

*Band Today,* Book 2, J. Ployhar, Student pages 11, 13–16, 18–21, 25, 26.
*Band Today,* Book 3, J. Ployhar, Student pages 19, 22.

### Music

"Blue Note Rhapsody," Lauder, Level I/II (includes fast $\frac{6}{8}$ section)
"L'il Gabriel," Dedrick, Level II (includes fast $\frac{6}{8}$ march)
"Main Theme from Star Trek," Goldsmith/Balent, Level II (fast $\frac{6}{8}$ with rests)
"Vive La Compagnie," Balent, Level I/II (fast $\frac{6}{8}$ )
"When Johnny Comes Marching Home," Ployhar, Level II ( $\frac{6}{8}$ with a contrasting $\frac{4}{4}$ middle)
"Theme from Superman," Williams/Lowden, Level II ( $\frac{12}{8}$ and sixteenth subdivision)

# Rhythm—Meter

## Specific Skill or Concept: $\frac{3}{8}$ *in 3*
## Performance Level: *I / II*

## Suggested Activities or Strategies

| Instructional Sequence | Techniques/Devices | Checks |
| --- | --- | --- |
| **1.** Explain $\frac{3}{8}$ time signature. | **1.** Use $\frac{3}{8}$ designation. | **1.** Make sure students can distinguish music in $\frac{3}{8}$ from music not in $\frac{3}{8}$, aurally and visually. |
| **2.** Students count aloud to three while they conduct a three-beat pattern. | **2.** Explain bottom number of time signature by putting the number one over the bottom number to create a fraction. This fraction, $\frac{1}{8}$, becomes the note receiving one pulse. | **2.** Have students demonstrate understanding and knowledge of note pyramid and duration relationships. |
| **3.** Students should count and play various rhythms, found in assigned literature, with a $\frac{3}{8}$ time signature. | **3.** Students set up a note pyramid, showing note durations. | **3.** Have students demonstrate understanding and knowledge of accented beats. |
| **4.** Students count aloud to three while conducting a three-beat pattern. Emphasize beat one. | **4.** Students echo rhythms with a $\frac{3}{8}$ time signature. | |
| **5.** Students should perform literature with a $\frac{3}{8}$ time signature, in three. | **5.** Students compose short compositions in $\frac{3}{8}$ time. | |

## Suggested Materials

### Texts or Methods

*Band Plus,* Book 2, J. Swearingen and B. Buehlman, 38.

# Melody—Melodic Notation/Terminology

## Specific Skill or Concept: *Glissando*
## Performance Level: *III / IV*

## Suggested Activities or Strategies

| Instructional Sequence | Techniques/Devices | Checks |
|---|---|---|
| **1.** Play recorded examples of pieces containing glissandi for various instruments. | ■ Give definition and explanation during rehearsal of a piece containing glissandi. | ■ Check for smooth execution from start to end. |
| **2.** Demonstrate technique involved in performing glissandi. | | |
| **3.** Drill the interval outlining glissando. | | |
| **4.** Work with students individually during lessons on performing glissandi on their instruments. | | |
| **5.** Measure student understanding on term test and/or playing test. | | |

## Suggested Materials

### Texts or Methods

*New Harvard Dictionary of Music,* D. Randel

### Music

"Lassus Trombone," Fillmore, Level III/IV
"Rhapsody in Blue," Gershwin/Grofé, Level III/IV

### Recordings

"A Salute to Henry Fillmore," Golden Crest CRS-4112.
"Rhapsody in Blue," Crest CRS-41288.

# Melody—Key Signatures

## Specific Skill or Concept: *c minor*
## Performance Level: *I / II*

## Suggested Activities or Strategies

| Instructional Sequence | Techniques/Devices | Checks |
|---|---|---|
| **1.** Establish minor tonality—I (Cm), V (Gm), I (Cm). | **1.** Play chords c minor, g minor, c minor on the keyboard. Say "minor tonality." | |
| **2.** Sing c natural minor scale to students on neutral syllable such as *bum*, ascending and descending at ♩ = 100. | **2.** Sing a cappella and have student echo you. | |
| **3.** Sing c minor scale to students using tonal syllables such as *la, ti, do,* ascending and descending at ♩ = 100. | **3.** Sing a cappella and have student echo you. | |
| **4.** Establish tonality; have student perform c minor scale on instruments at ♩ = 100. | **4.** Focus on intonation. Sing through the instrument. | |
| **5.** Notate c minor signature on board in both treble and bass clefs. | **5.** Draw an arrow pointing toward C *(la)*. | |

## Suggested Materials

**Music**

"Kings Go Forth," O'Reilly, Level I/II

# Harmony—Tonal Systems

## Specific Skill or Concept: *Dorian / Mixolydian / Other Modes*
## Performance Level: *III / IV*

*Note: Modes are best introduced after the concepts major and minor are understood. Dorian and other modes should be presented when students encounter them in music such as folk songs or jazz.*

## Suggested Activities or Strategies

| Instructional Sequence | Techniques/Devices | Checks |
|---|---|---|

*Dorian Mode*

**1.** Point out that scales may begin on any degree of the (major) scale and that these modes were once widely used.

**2.** Have the students vocalize and play the Dorian scale. Present examples of it in music of band, ensembles, and folksongs such as "And the Trees Do Moan" (folk carol) and older versions of "Greensleeves" (later versions may be written in melodic minor).

**3.** Have the students write melodies in this mode, both in pure form and with the raised seventh in the cadential formula.

**4.** For greater command of this mode, have the students vocalize drills in which note or notes of the scale are left out and the students "hear" the pitch internally and proceed to the next audible pitch.

*Other Modes*

**1.** Introduce these scales when encountered in music.

**2.** Students should vocalize and play the scales. Present examples of the scale in music and indicate value of knowing it and recognizing it in jazz.

**3.** Have the students utilize each scale in jazz performance and in improvisation.

**4.** Have the students write music utilizing this mode and others.

## Suggested Materials

### Music

Folksongs, jazz method books, or Christmas medleys containing "Greensleeves."

# Harmony—Other Harmonic Concepts

### Specific Skill or Concept: *Progression*
### Performance Level: *IV/V*

## Suggested Activities or Strategies

| Instructional Sequence | Techniques/Devices | Checks |
|---|---|---|
| **1.** Students experience aurally several different kinds of progressions. | **1. a.** Demonstrate through recordings or band performance the idea of harmonic progression as opposed to static harmony.<br><br>**b.** You may wish to demonstrate retrogression or parallel harmony as opposed to standard progressions (such as down a fifth, up a second, down a third). | |
| **2.** Students perform progressions in band pieces being studied. | **2.** Students perform progressions in pieces they are studying. | **2.** Scan the class to keep all students focused on discussion. |
| **3.** Students summarize reasons for progression. | **3.** Encourage students to come up with aesthetic reasons for progression. A list on board or overhead may include forward motion of piece, relief from harmonic fatigue, different "colors," etc. A short demonstration of cadence progressions would immediately show the aesthetic effects of perfect cadence (V-I) as opposed to a deceptive cadence (V-VI). | **3.** Do not allow discussion to bog down. End the lesson by playing and encourage students to feel the aesthetic effect of progression (assuming a correct and beautiful performance). |

## Suggested Materials

### Texts or Methods

*Chorale Time,* Vol. 1 and 2, L. Chidester
*Forty-Two Chorales,* P. Gordon

### Music

"The Engulfed Cathedral," Debussy/Longfield, Level IV (example of parallel harmonies)

# Form—Compositional Devices

## Specific Skill or Concept: *Homophony*
## Performance Level: *I*

## Suggested Activities or Strategies

| Instructional Sequence | Techniques/Devices | Checks |
| --- | --- | --- |
| **1.** Rehearse sample composition in two groups—sections with the melody; sections with chordal foundation.<br><br>**2.** Explain compositional techniques of horizontal and vertical composition.<br><br>**3.** Combine all sections to demonstrate total sound of homophony. | ■ Homorhythmic: Remind students that all of the musicians are playing alike rhythmically, which allows them to listen for harmonic balance and creates a sense of teamwork.<br><br>■ Melody with harmonic accompaniment: This is a typical device of the classical period. The accompaniment supports the melody but is weak on its own. Have the melody parts play. Have the rest of the ensemble play without the melody. Have the students imagine that the melody is being played and see if the accompaniment guides the listener in the path of the melody. | |

## Suggested Materials

### Texts or Methods

*Encore!* Book I, B. Pearson, Student Book, 15 #43; 11 #28.
*Belwin Comprehensive Band Method,* Book I, F. Erickson

### Music

"The Crusaders," Erickson, Level I
"Mozart Musicale," Williams, Level I
"Festival," Erickson, Level I
"Simple Gifts," traditional/Tyler, Level I

# Form—Compositional Structures

## Specific Skill or Concept: *Theme and Variation*
## Performance Level: *II / III*

### Suggested Activities or Strategies

| Instructional Sequence | Techniques/Devices | Checks |
|---|---|---|
| | Discuss rhythmic, harmonic, and melodic changes on a given theme, usually in sectional form. | |

### Suggested Materials

#### Music

"Variations on a Theme by Mozart," McGinty, Level II
"The Drunken Sailor," Hull, Level II/III
"Variation Overture," Williams, Level II/III
"God of Our Fathers," Smith, Level III/IV
"Symphonic Variations on Amazing Grace," Smith, Level III/IV
"Variations on Joy to the World," Christensen, Level IV
"Variations on a Korean Folk Song," Chance, Level IV/V
"Variants on a Medieval Tune," Dello Joio, Level V
"The Earle of Oxford's March," Byrd/Jacobs, Level V
"Variations on a Hymn by Louis Bourgeois," Smith, Level V
"Festival Variations," Smith, Level VI
"Theme & Variations, Op. 43a," Schoenberg, Level VI

# Timbre/Texture

## Specific Skill or Concept: *Orchestration*
## Performance Level: *II / III*

### Suggested Activities or Strategies

| Instructional Sequence | Techniques/Devices | Checks |
| --- | --- | --- |
| **1.** Play recording of composition that demonstrates various orchestrations. Students listen and discuss the examples. | | |
| **2.** Introduce literature that exemplifies various types of orchestration. Ask students to balance the ensemble sounds of the various orchestrations. | | |
| **3.** Introduce more than one example of the same piece orchestrated differently by other composers. | | |

### Suggested Materials

**Music**

"Quintagon," Frackenpohl, Level II/III
"Irish Tune from County Derry," Grainger, Level III

# Expression—Articulation

## Specific Skill or Concept: *Legato*
## Peformance Level: *I / II*

### Suggested Activities or Strategies

| Instructional Sequence | Techniques/Devices | Checks |
| --- | --- | --- |
| **1.** Students tongue set of quarter notes. | **1.** Students say *ta ta ta ta* for regular tonguing, compared to *doo doo doo doo* for legato tonguing. | **1.** Make sure there is no change in embouchure. Air stream must remain constant. Student should keep air moving. |
| **2.** Students tongue the same set of quarter notes but make them sound as smooth as possible. | **2.** Play quarter notes on each scale degree. Alternate legato and regular tonguing between scale degrees. | |
| **3.** Introduce the term legato as meaning "smooth and connected." | **3.** Compare staccato and legato articulations as opposites:<br><br>♩ ♩ ♩ ♩ ♩ ♩ ♩ ♩<br><br>staccato    legato | |
| **4.** Play an étude or piece that reinforces legato articulation. | | |

### Suggested Materials

#### Texts or Methods

*Best in Class,* B. Pearson, Student Book II, 9.

#### Music

"Theme from Finlandia," Sibelius/Huffnagel, Level I/II
"All Through the Night," Henderson/Stoutamire, Level I/II
"Andantino," Khachaturian/Henderson, Level I/II

# Historical Information

# Historical Information

The emphasis for these concepts is not the actual instructional process for teaching the concepts, but rather suggested materials and music that can be used to enhance understanding. The process actually involves learning the concept through band performance. It is strongly suggested that the instructor supplement these concepts by using examples from orchestral repertoire and creating traditional teaching plans relative to the specific concept. For a complete listing of historical concepts to be introduced, see the *Skills and Concepts—Recommended Performance Levels* section. A sample plan for teaching a historical concept follows.

# Composers

## Specific Skill or Concept: *John Philip Sousa*
## Performance Level: *II*

## Suggested Activities or Strategies

| Instructional Sequence | Techniques/Devices | Checks |
| --- | --- | --- |

■ Discuss historical information about John Philip Sousa and the Sousa Band.

■ Refer to text and video sources below.

■ Perform appropriate-level Sousa march.

## Suggested Materials

### Texts or Methods

*Band Music Notes,* N. Smith and A. Stoutamire
*March Music Notes,* N. Smith

### Music

"Sousa Spectacular," Schaffer, Level II
"Semper Fidelis," Sousa/Osterling, Level II
"The Liberty Bell," Sousa/Osterling, Level II
"King Cotton," Sousa/Keller, Level II
"Sousa Sounds," Balent, Level II
"The Thunderer," Sousa/Osterling, Level II
"March King Medley," Sousa/Schaeffer, Level II
"Sounds of Sousa," Ployhar, Level II
"The Stars and Stripes Forever," Sousa/Curnow, Level II
"High School Cadets," Sousa/Gore, Level III
Any original Sousa march

### Videotapes

*The New Sousa Band on Stage at Wolf Trap,* Keith Brion, conductor (Proscenium Entertainment)
*The History of Bands in America* (Sirs Music)

# Creativity and Valuing Concepts

# Creativity and Valuing Concepts

Creativity and valuing concepts are undoubtedly the most difficult for educators to approach. They often involve skills that require extensive prerequisite learning or are involved with outcomes that are difficult to observe and measure. For these reasons, they are often the most frequently neglected.

The philosophical position of this course of study is that educators must include these items in the daily teaching and learning process. Teachers must not ignore these concepts simply because they are difficult. Inclusion is critical because creating and valuing concepts are a *basic* part of our art form—an art form that is unique and that cannot be replicated in any other facet of a student's education. Therefore, it is incumbent upon all educators to understand these concepts and create an educational environment during band study where they can flourish. For a complete listing of the creativity and valuing concepts that should be introduced, see the *Skills and Concepts—Recommended Performance Levels* section. Sample plans for teaching creativity and valuing concepts follow.

# Improvisation

## Specific Skill or Concept: *Solo/Cadenza*
## Performance Level: *III*

## Suggested Activities or Strategies

| Instructional Sequence | Techniques/Devices | Checks |
| --- | --- | --- |

*Students should be well versed in chord structure and progressions.*

| Instructional Sequence | Techniques/Devices | Checks |
| --- | --- | --- |
| **1.** Review key of song being used. | **1.** Use only chord tones at first. | ■ Check phrasing. |
| **2.** Review and analyze the progression underlying the cadenza. | **2.** Have students visualize the chord tones. | ■ Make sure cadenza ends on consonant sound. |
| **3.** Discuss rhythmic variations, melodic variations, such as scalewise, intervallic leaps, upper and lower neighboring tones, consonant and dissonant note choices. | **3.** Encourage rhythmic, melodic, and dynamic variations. | |
| **4.** Perform cadenza for student, if possible with student playing chord progression. | **4.** Demonstrate the melodic pattern with lines. Ex.: | |
| **5.** Have student perform while the teacher plays the chord progression. |  | |

## Suggested Materials

### Texts or Methods

"Cadenza," *New Harvard Dictionary of Music,* D. Randel

### Music

Any instrument solo/cadenza

# Valuing

## Specific Skill/Concept: *Discrimination*
## Performance Level: *I / II*

## Suggested Activities or Strategies

| Instructional Sequence | Techniques/Devices | Checks |
| --- | --- | --- |
| **1.** Introduce students to music through recordings or live performances that display a creditable level of music as an art form.<br><br>**2.** Introduce students to music that has historical significance and is relative to these performance skills. | | **1.** Students' reaction to listening experience should show an accepting attitude.<br><br>**2.** Students should display positive attitudes toward the class as evidenced by participation and improved skills in performance and discrimination. |

## Suggested Materials

### Texts or Methods

*Dimensions of Musical Thinking,* E. Boardman, ed.
*Dimensions of Thinking: A Framework for Curriculum and Instruction*
*Aesthetic Education: What It Means and Why It Matters,* B. Reimer

# Appendix

## Texts and Methods

*Advanced Fun with Fundamentals*, B. Laas and F. Weber (Belwin-Mills)
*Advanced Rubank Method (Clarinet)*, H. Voxman and W. Gower (Rubank)
*Aesthetic Education: What It Means and Why It Matters*, B. Reimer (Music Educators National Conference)
*Alfred's Basic Band Method*, S. Feldstein and J. O'Reilly (Alfred)
*Alfred's New Band Method*, S. Feldstein (Alfred)
*The Art of Bassoon Playing*, W. Spencer (Summy-Birchard)
*The Art of Brass Playing*, P. Farkas (Wind Music, Inc.)
*The Art of Electronic Music* (G.P.I. Publications)
*The Art of Flute Playing*, E. Putnik (Summy-Birchard)
*The Art of French Horn Playing*, P. Farkas (Summy-Birchard)
*The Art of Oboe Playing*, R. Sprenkle and D. Ledet (Summy-Birchard)
*The Art of Saxophone Playing*, L. Teal (Summy-Birchard)
*The Art of Trombone Playing*, E. Kleinhammer (Summy-Birchard)

*Band Encounters*, J. Swearingen and B. Buehlman (Heritage Music)
*Band Fundamentals*, M. Taylor (Belwin-Mills)
*Band Magic*, F. Erickson (Belwin-Mills)
*Band Method*, E. Sueta (Macie Publishing)
*Band Music Guide* (The Instrumentalist Company)
*Band Music Notes*, N. Smith and A. Stoutamire (Program Note Press)
*Band Plus*, J. Swearingen and B. Buehlman (Heritage Music)
*Band Today*, J. Ployhar (CPP/Belwin)
*Bands Away*, J. Ployhar and E. Osterling et al. (Belwin-Mills)
*Band-Sembles in Concert*, F. Erickson (Belwin-Mills)
*The Beacon Band Method*, H. Bennett (Beacon Music)
*Belwin Band Builder*, W. Douglas and F. Weber (Belwin-Mills)
*Belwin Comprehensive Band Method*, F. Erickson (Belwin-Mills)
*Belwin Elementary Band Method*, F. Weber (Belwin-Mills)
*Best in Class*, B. Pearson (Kjos)
*Brass Anthology* (The Instrumentalist Company)
*Breeze-Easy Method*, J. Kinyon (M. Witmark and Sons)
*Building Tomorrow's Band...Today!* J. Burden (Columbia Pictures Publications)

*Chorale Time*, L. Chidester (Carl Fischer)
*Clarinet Student*, F. Weber and R. Lowry (Belwin-Mills)
*A Creative Approach to the French Horn*, H. Berv (Theodore Presser)
*The Creative Director: Alternative Rehearsal Techniques*, E. Lisk (Meredith Music)

*Dimensions of Musical Thinking*, E. Boardman, ed. (Music Educators National Conference)
*Dimensions of Thinking: A Framework for Curriculum and Instruction* (Association for Supervision and
    Curriculum Development)

*Effective Performance of Band Music*, W. McBeth (Southern Music Company)
*Encore! Best in Class Series*, B. Pearson (Kjos)
*Exercises For Ensemble Drill*, R. Fussell (Belwin-Mills)

*First Division Band Method*, F. Weber (Belwin-Mills)
*Forty-Two Chorales*, P. Gordon (Bourne)
*Fourteen Weeks to a Better Band*, R. Maxwell (C. L. Barnhouse)
*Fun with Fundamentals*, B. Laas and F. Weber (Belwin-Mills)

*Guide to Teaching Brass*, N. Hunt (William C. Brown)
*Guide to Teaching Woodwinds*, F. Westphal (William C. Brown)
*Guide to Teaching Percussion*, R. Holloway and H. Bartlett (William C. Brown)

*Hal Freese Advanced Band Method,* H. Freese (Belwin-Mills)
*Hal Freese Elementary Band Method,* H. Freese (Belwin-Mills)
*Hal Freese Intermediate Band Method,* H. Freese (Belwin-Mills)
*Hal Leonard Intermediate Band Method,* H. Rusch (Hal Leonard)

*The Individualized Instructor,* J. Froseth (G.I.A. Publications)
*Intermediate Drum Method,* R. Burns and S. Feldstein (Belwin-Mills)
*Intermediate Steps to the Band,* M. Taylor (Belwin-Mills)

*Jump Right In: The Instrumental Series,* R. Grunow and E. Gordon (G.I.A. Publications)

*Learning Unlimited Band Method,* A. Jenson (Hal Leonard)

*March Music Notes,* N. Smith (Program Note Press)
*Master Studies,* J. Morello (Modern Drummer Publications)
*Melodious Etudes for Trombone,* M. Bordagni and J. Rochut (Carl Fischer)
*The MIDI Book: Using MIDI and Related Interfaces,* S. DeFuria (Third Earth Productions)
*MIDI for Musicians,* C. Anderton (Amsco Publications)
*Modern Rudimental Swing Solos,* C. Wilcoxon (Chas. S. Wilcoxon)
*Music and the Macintosh,* G. Yelton (MIDI America)
*Music Education—Aesthetic Education: In the Real World of the School,* B. Reimer (Music Educators National
     Conference)
*Music for Young Woodwinds, Our First Clarinet Book,* H. Van Lijnschooten (Heritage Music)
*Music Through MIDI,* M. Broom (Microsoft Press)

*The New Harvard Dictionary of Music,* D. Randel (The Belknap Press of Harvard University)
*Note Grouping,* J. Thurmond (Meredith Music)

*The Oboe Revealed,* C. Sawicki (Box 401, Delhi, NY 13753)

*Practical Hints on Playing the Saxophone,* E. Rousseau (Belwin-Mills)
*Prime Time,* F. Erickson and E. Osterling et al. (Belwin-Mills)

*Rehearsal Fundamentals,* F. Weber (Belwin-Mills)
*Rehearsal Handbook for Band and Orchestra Students,* R. Garofalo (Meredith Music)
*Rubank Method,* H. Voxman and W. Gower (Rubank)

*Selective Music Lists 1971* (Music Educators National Conference)
*Selective Music List for Bands* (National Band Association)
*Sessions in Sound,* B. Buehlman and K. Whitcomb (Heritage Music)
*Stick Control,* G. Stone (George B. Stone & Son)
*Symphonic Warm-Ups for Band,* C. Smith (Jenson)

*Teaching Instrumental Music,* R. Colwell (Prentice Hall)
*Teaching Percussion,* G. Cook (Macmillan)
*Technique Today,* J. Ployhar (Belwin-Mills)
*Treasury of Scales,* L. Smith (CPP/Belwin)

*Visual Band Method,* V. Leidig and L. Niehaus (Highland/Etling)

*Woodwinds,* G. Saucier (Macmillan)

*Yamaha Band Student,* S. Feldstein and J. O'Reilly (Alfred)

## Music

"Aevia," Curnow (Musicworks) Level III
"Air and Alleluia," Mozart/Kinyon (Alfred) Level II
"Air for Band," Erickson (Bourne) Level II
"Air for Winds," Shelton (Ludwig) Level II/III
"All Through the Night," Henderson/Stoutamire (Lake State Publications) Level I/II
"Alpha and Omega," Yoder (Marks) Level III/IV
"American Civil War Fantasy," Bilik (Southern Music) Level IV/V
"American Folk Rhapsody No. 3," Grundman (Boosey & Hawkes) Level III
"American Pioneer Suite," Fox (Pro Art Publications) Level III
"Americans We," Fillmore/Balent (Carl Fischer) Level II
"Americans We," Fillmore (Carl Fischer) Level III/IV
"Andantino," Khachaturian/Henderson (Pro Art Publications) Level I/II
"Anthem for Winds and Percussion," Smith (Jenson) Level III
"Aria (When Thou Art Near)," Bach/Nowak (BBI) Level II
"Armed Forces on Parade," Balent (Carl Fischer)
"Astro Overture," Kinyon (Alfred) Level II
"At the Summit (Concert March)," Nowak (Charing Cross) Level II
"Aventura," Swearingen (Barnhouse) Level II/III

"Beethoven's Fifth Symphony," Beethoven/Kinyon (Alfred) Level II
"The Black Watch," Smith (Jenson) Level III
"Block M," Bilik (Mills Music) Level IV
"Blue Note Rhapsody," Lauder (Alfred) Level I/II
"Brighton Beach," Latham (Summy-Birchard) Level III

"Canzona," Mennin (Bourne) Level IV
"Castles in Spain," Erickson (Belwin-Mills) Level I
"Chorale and Alleluia," Hanson (Carl Fischer) Level IV
"Chorale and Canon," Del Borgo (Kendor) Level II
"Color," Margolis (Manhattan Beach) Level IV/V
"Conversation for Band," Kinyon (Alfred) Level I/II
"The Crusaders," Erickson ( elwin-Mills) Level I

"The Drunken Sailor," Hull (Wynn) Level II/III

"The Earle of Oxford's March," Byrd/Jacobs (Boosey & Hawkes) Level V
"El Capitan," Sousa (Church) Level III
"The Engulfed Cathedral," Debussy/Longfield (Barnhouse) Level IV
"Epinicion," Paulson (Kjos) Level IV

"The Fairest of the Fair," Sousa (Church) Level III
"Fantasia in G," Mahr (Kjos) Level IV
"Fantasy for Horn," Arnold (Faber Music Co.) Level IV
"Festival," in *Away We Go,* Erickson (Belwin-Mills) Level I
"A Festival Prelude," Reed (Marks) Level III
"Festival Variations," Smith (Wingert-Jones) Level VI
"Festivo," Nehlybel (Belwin-Mills) Level III
"Finale from Water Music," Handel/Shaffer (Heritage Music) Level II/III
"Finale to William Tell Overture," Rossini/Balent (Carl Fischer) Level II
"First Suite in E♭" (Revised), Holst (Boosey & Hawkes) Level IV
"Flourish for Wind Band," Vaughan Williams (Oxford) Level III

"God of Our Fathers," Smith (Wingert-Jones) Level III/IV
"The Golden Shield," Nowak (BBI) Level III
"Greensleeves," Reed, arr. (Hal Leonard) Level III

"The Headless Horseman," Broege (Alaire) Level III
"High School Cadets," Sousa/Gore (Belwin-Mills) Level III
"Howard Hanson Suite," Balent, arr. (Carl Fischer) Level II
"Hymn of Brotherhood," Beethoven/Tolmage (Staff) Level II
"Hymn of Freedom," Brahms/Gardner (Staff) Level II/III

"Instant Concert," Walters (Rubank) Level III
"Irish Tune from County Derry," Grainger (G. Schirmer) Level III

"Japanese Fantasy," Erickson (Belwin-Mills) Level II/III

"Kentucky 1800," Grundman (Boosey & Hawkes) Level II
"King Cotton," Sousa/Keller (Wynn) Level II
"Kings Go Forth," O'Reilly (Alfred) Level I/II
"Korean Folk Rhapsody," Curnow (Jenson) Level II

"Lassus Trombone," Fillmore (Fillmore Bros.) Level III/IV
"The Liberty Bell," Sousa/Osterling (Jensen) Level II
"Lincolnshire Posy," Grainger (Ludwig/G. Schirmer) Level VI
"Londonderry Air," Kinyon (Alfred) Level I/II
"L'il Gabriel," Dedrick (Kendor) Level II

"Main Theme from Star Trek," Goldsmith/Balent (Warner Bros.) Level II
"March from Symphony No. 6," Tchaikovsky/Balent (Carl Fischer) Level III
"March Grandioso," Seitz/Reed (Southern) Level III/IV
"March Juno," Stewart (Shawnee) Level III
"March King Medley," Sousa/Schaeffer (Barnhouse) Level II
"March on an Irish Air," Smith (Jenson) Level III
"Military Escort," Bennett/Fennell (Carl Fischer) Level II
"The Mission," Williams/Lavender (Jenson) Level IV
"Monticello Overture," McGinty (Barnhouse) Level II
"Moorside March," Holst/Curnow (Jenson) Level III
"Morceau de Concert Op. 94," Saint Säens (Warner Brothers Music) Level IV
"Mozart Musicale," Williams (Shapiro, Bernstein, and Co.) Level I
"Music for Prague 1968," Husa (AMP) Level VI

"National Emblem March," Bagley (Carl Fischer) Level IV
"Nimrod," Elgar/Reed (Belwin-Mills) Level II/III
"Northwest Suite," O'Reilly (Alfred) Level II/III
"Novena," Swearingen (Barnhouse) Level III

"An Outdoor Overture," Copland (Boosey & Hawkes) Level V
"Overture in B♭," Giovannini/Robinson (Fox) Level III/IV

"Pageant," Persichetti (Carl Fischer) Level IV
"Paul Revere's Ride," Yoder (Hanson) Level III

"Quintagon," Frackenpohl (Elkan-Vogel) Level II/III

"Rakes of Mallow," Anderson (Kalmus) Level III/IV
"Reflections," Swearingen (Barnhouse) Level II/III
"Religioso," Nehlybel (Alfred) Level II
"Rhapsody in Blue," Gershwin/Grofé (Harms) Level III/IV
"Rhosymedre," Williams/Beeler (Galaxy) Level III

"Sakura, Sakura," Ployhar, arr. (Belwin-Mills) Level I
"Scarborough Fair," MacBeth, arr. (Alfred) Level II
"Second Suite in F" (Revised), Holst (Boosey & Hawkes) Level V
"Selections from the King and I," Rodgers and Hammerstein/Bennett (Williamson) Level IV
"Semper Fidelis," Sousa/Osterling (Belwin-Mills) Level II
"Simple Gifts," traditional/Tyler (Alfred) Level I
"Sonatina for Band," Erickson (Bourne) Level II
"Songs of the Sea," Kinyon (Alfred) Level I/II
"Sounds of Sousa," Ployhar (Belwin-Mills) Level II
"Sousa Sounds," Balent (Carl Fischer) Level II
"Sousa Spectacular," Schaffer (C. L. Barnhouse) Level II
"The Stars and Stripes Forever," Sousa/Curnow (Jenson) Level II
"Starship One," Chattaway (William Allen Music) Level I
"Suite Modale," McGinty (Queenwood Publications) Level II
"Suite of Old American Dances," Bennett (Chappell) Level V

"Symphonic Variations on Amazing Grace," Smith (Jenson) Level III/IV

"Thanksgiving Hymn," Laubach (BBI) Level II/III
"Them Basses," Huffine and Balent (Carl Fischer) Level III
"Theme from Finlandia," Sibelius/Huffnagle (Pro Art Publications) Level I/II
"Theme from Superman," Williams/Lowden (Warner Bros.) Level II
"The Thunderer," Sousa/Osterling (Jenson) Level II
"Theme & Variations, Op. 43a," Schoenberg (G. Schirmer) Level VI
"Three Kentucky Sketches," O'Reilly (Alfred) Level II
"Three Pieces for Winds," Edmondson (Jenson) Level III/IV
"Two Hebrew Folk Songs," Ward, arr. (Kendor) Level II/III

"Ukrainian Bell Carol," Balent, arr. (Warner Bros.) Level II

"Valdres Concert March," Hansen/Curnow (Jenson) Level III
"Variants on a Medieval Tune," Dello Joio (Marks) Level V
"Variation Overture,"  Williams (Ludwig) Level II/III
"Variations on a Hymn by Louis Bourgeois," Smith (Jenson) Level V
"Variations on a Korean Folk Song," Chance (Boosey & Hawkes) Level IV/V
"Variations on a Theme by Mozart," McGinty (Hal Leonard) Level II
"Variations on Joy to the World," Christensen (Kendor) Level IV
"Villanelle," Dukas (Durand & Co.) Level IV
"Vive la Compagnie," Balent, arr. (Warner Bros.) Level I/II

"The Washington Post," Sousa (Carl Fischer) Level III/IV
"Watermelon Man," Hancock/Edmondson (Hal Leonard) Level II/III
"When Johnny Comes Marching Home," Ployhar, arr. (Byron Douglas) Level II
"William Byrd Suite," Jacob (Boosey & Hawkes) Level IV
"Wondrous Love," Ployhar (Carl Fischer) Level II

"Young Winners," Burden (Southern Music) Level II